SUMMER *in Santa Fe*

SUMMER
in Santa Fe

GARDEN-FRESH MENUS FROM THE CITY DIFFERENT

Culinary Text, Recipes, and Menus by

Janet Mitchell

General Text and Photographs by

Johanna Omelia

GIBBS·SMITH
PUBLISHER

SALT LAKE CITY

For Jeff Mitchell,

best friend and husband

extraordinaire, who is

willing to try just about

anything I cook.

—*Janet Mitchell*

To the original inhabitants

of The Old Monastery,

Santa Fe, who, a century

ago, planted the fruit trees,

flowers and herbs that

provided the inspiration

for this book.

—*Johanna Omelia*

First Edition
05 04 03 02 01   5 4 3 2 1

Culinary text, recipes, and menus copyright © 2001 by Janet Mitchell
General text and photographs copyright © 2001 by Johanna Omelia

Woodblock prints by Willard F. Clark—courtesy Kevin Ryan, Santa Fe, New Mexico
Historical photos—courtesy The Museum of New Mexico:
> *Baking Bread in Horno*, San Ildefonso Pueblo, Neg. No. 3712 [p. 19]
> *Artists at Work*, photo by Wesley Bradford, Neg. No. 13325 [p. 29]
> *Albuquerque Truck Garden*, Neg. No. 5158 [p. 45]
> *Grinding Corn*, San Juan Pueblo, photo by T. Harmon Parkhurst, Neg. No. 3964 [p. 59]
> *Cowboys Going to Dinner*, Neg. No. 5324 [p. 75]
> *Picnic Cooking*, Neg. No. 112674 [p. 89]
> *Agriculture Display*, photo by J. R. Riddle, Neg. No. 76049 [p. 101]
> *Husking Corn*, photo by Ed Andrews, Neg. No. 71218 [p. 115]
> *Fiesta Trouvadores*, photo by A. J. Baker, Neg. No. 52885 [p. 129]

Published by
Gibbs Smith, Publisher
P.O. Box 667
Layton, Utah 84041

Orders: (1-800) 748-5439
www.gibbs-smith.com

Edited by Linda Nimori
Designed by FORTHGEAR, Inc.
Printed and bound in Korea

Library of Congress Cataloging-in-Publication Data

Mitchell, Janet, 1941–
    Summer in Santa Fe : garden-fresh menus from the City Different / Janet Mitchell and Johanna Omelia.— 1st ed.
        p. cm.
        ISBN 0-87905-967-2
            1. Cookery, American—Southwestern style. 2. Cookery—New Mexico—Santa Fe.
            3. Santa Fe (N.M.)—Social life and customs. 4. Santa Fe (N.M.)—History.
            I. Omelia, Johanna, 1959– II. Title.
        TX715.2.S69 M58 2001
        641.59789'56—dc21
                                                                00-063567

Acknowledgments

The writers would like to thank the following people whose contributions to this book are invaluable.

A big heartfelt thanks from Janet Mitchell to Jeff Mitchell and the many friends and family members who have contributed their enthusiasm, inspiration and love throughout the writing of this book. Gratitude also to computer genius Stella Davidsen, historian Nancy Lopez, and Jan and Kathy Nelson for use of their lovely garden for photography. Sincere thanks to Lori Delapp, Mari Moga and Susan Thomas for their recipe-testing expertise. Kudos to the many scholarly food writers, dedicated cooks and serious students who take pride in celebrating the virtues of homemade food.

Johanna Omelia thanks editor and gifted poet Mary Jane Tenerelli, England's best proofreader Ian Jones, New Mexico historian Lee Goodwin, artist Catherine Sobredo, artist Bryony Bensly, food editor Lisa Miller, Jim and Terri May, and Lisa Thomen for providing a delightful picnic venue in Pecos. Thanks to the folks at the Farmers' Market for their information on local farms and crops, and to Michael Waldock for his enthusiasm and support.

We'd both like to thank our models—the beautiful Isabel Tapia, Adrian Sinaloa, baritone Kurt Ollmann, Mary Jo Hopson, Ermenda Martinez, and Jack Precht. A special thanks to Madge Baird and Linda Nimori for meticulous editing.

Contents

New Mexico Culture and Cuisine

New Mexico's history is unique compared to the rest of the United States. Before gaining statehood in 1912, the area saw millennia of Indian civilizations, 250 years of Colonial Spanish and Mexican rule, trappers and traders, pioneers and cowboys. The dramatic and beautiful mountain landscape continues to attract a variety of visitors who come to enjoy the culturally diverse tastes and traditions of the area as well as its world-renowned cuisine.

History, Food and Drink

About two thousand years ago, the Anasazi, ancestors of today's Pueblo Indians, settled along the fertile banks and valleys of the Rio Grande. The Pueblo people were farmers; corn, beans and squash were their three major crops and remain so today. Wild plants, native seeds, nuts and berries supplemented their diets, along with wild game–deer, elk, antelope and rabbit. Archeological discoveries have also uncovered turkey pens, indicating that the Pueblo Indians domesticated turkeys as a food source.

Traditionally, food has held great spiritual significance for the Pueblo Indians. Feast days are holy events. Corn in particular is more than a crop to the Pueblo people. All Rio Grande Pueblo peoples perform the Corn Dance: a ceremony danced by an entire population of a Pueblo (village)–a prayer to ensure the consistent cultivation and propagation of corn. Some tribes refer to the sun as "father" and the earth as "mother"; corn is also called "mother." Stories of the Corn Mother and the Corn Maiden feature heavily in creation myths and remain an integral part of the religious ritual. While crop dances take place in the spring and summer, animal dances are usually performed in the winter months.

In 1540, Spanish explorer Francisco Vasquez de Coronado led an expedition into southern New Mexico, searching for the Cities of Gold. He reportedly arrived with a thousand stallions and as many head of cattle.

In 1598, Don Juan de Oñate ventured into northern New Mexico with soldiers, priests and farmers to settle the northernmost outpost of New Spain. About 1607, Don Pedro de Peralta arrived in Santa Fe and settled here, making it the new capital of the province. The Plaza was quickly established as the heart of the city, which the Spanish named "Holy Faith." The Palace of the Governors was built to house Peralta and his staff and remains the oldest continually used government building in the United States. Over hundreds of years, the Plaza has served as a public marketplace, a grazing field, an army barracks and the site of bloody battles.

Gradually, the Spanish introduced domesticated animals such as cattle, sheep, goats, pigs, geese, ducks and chickens into the region, providing new food sources. Wheat was another important Spanish contribution, as were a wealth of herbs that were often prized for their curative powers and their ability to enhance the flavor of foods.

The Europeans established orchards in Santa Fe. Ancient fruit trees, including apricot, pear and apple, are still growing all over town despite infrequent rain and the high altitude. Dried plums, raisins and wild currants were popular sweeteners and were added to desserts, sausages and other foods. To provide water for their crops, orchards and stock, the people of New Spain built *acequias,* or irrigation ditches. The water was gathered from rain as well as snow runoff from the Sangre de Cristos and was also diverted from local rivers and arroyos. The network of acequias dug by farmers in the seventeenth century is still apparent on the famous Canyon Road and Acequia Madre, the road that runs parallel to Canyon Road.

In 1680, the Pueblo Indians banded together, drove the Spanish out and took over the Palace of the Governors. They settled in Santa Fe until twelve years later when Don Diego de Vargas recaptured the city, an event commemorated by Fiestas de Santa Fe.

During the next century, Santa Fe became an important center of trade along the Camino Real that ran from Santa Fe to Mexico City. In 1821, Mexico won independence from Spain. Subsequently, the Santa Fe Trail opened up and covered wagons from Missouri poured into the area. The new trading route brought prosperity to New Mexico and other important cultural influences as "Anglo" traders from a variety

of nations entered the region. In 1846, the United States went to war with Mexico and claimed the area from Texas to California as its territory.

When the railroads were constructed here around 1880, gastronomic specialties from both the East Coast and the West Coast became available. Tinned foods such as oysters and meats that were traded along the Santa Fe Trail were now available fresh. The railroad also brought immigrants from Europe, China and other countries whose tastes and skills impacted local cuisine and traditions.

Wine had as much religious significance to the early European immigrants as corn did to the Native Americans. Centuries ago, Franciscan monks brought sacramental wines to the region and began making their own wines for religious ceremonies. In the 1880s, French winemakers arrived by railroad and their skills moved the wine industry forward by leaps and bounds. Today, many fine wines are produced in New Mexico.

Years ago, the growing and preparation of food consumed the bulk of a New Mexico family's day. Planting and tending crops and livestock, milling and threshing wheat, stringing chile *ristras,* crushing grapes for wine–all were labor-intensive jobs, particularly arduous in this land of little water and temperature extremes.

In the last century, artists and writers moved to Santa Fe and immortalized the New Mexico landscape and its people. The quality of the light, the unique adobe architecture, and the mountain scenery continues to cast its spell, drawing visitors from around the world.

The Plaza remains the heart of Santa Fe. Such events as Spanish Market, Fiestas and Indian Market keep downtown buzzing with festive activity. Santa Fe's multi-cultural heritage is well documented in the wealth of museums attesting to the rich and fascinating history of the area. And, with more than 200 galleries, Santa Fe is the third largest art market in the country. Beyond the city, New Mexico remains the home of nineteen Pueblo villages, two Apache reservations and a portion of the Diné (Navajo) reservation. Nearby national parks feature Anasazi ruins and historical artifacts to explore as well as acres of beautiful scenery.

About Chiles

Chiles are widely used throughout the world's cuisines. With more than 1,600 varieties, chiles are used as a condiment, a spice and a vegetable, adding appealing flavor, color and zest to food. The centerpiece of contemporary New Mexico cuisine, chile peppers originated in South America, where the pre-Columbian Indians of the Americas grew them. It is believed that Captain General Don Juan de Oñate brought the first peppers to New Mexico in 1598.

The largest share of the world's chile crops is grown and consumed in New Mexico. It is estimated that the average New Mexico family eats forty pounds of chiles per year! Chiles are eaten in everything imaginable, from scrambled eggs to sushi, from drinks to desserts. Fresh New Mexico green chiles and dried New Mexico red chiles are the types most commonly used by Santa Fe cooks. They are one of the few varieties of chiles to keep the same name in both fresh and dried forms. The New Mexico chiles range between 1 (mild) and 6 (moderately hot) on the Scoville Heat Scale. These popular chiles, sometimes referred to as long greens and long reds, are a medium bright green before turning red in the fall, and measure 6 to 7 inches long.

The immature chile pods, which are eaten green, are harvested starting in August. In the fall, the ripe red chiles are left to dry on the plant, dried in ovens or strung into ristras. Long rows of brilliant red chile ristras silhouetted against adobe walls are a familiar sight in New Mexico. Many of the ristras sold in Santa Fe today are decorative and have been shellacked to maintain their bright color. Locals refer to red and green chile sauces served on the same plate as "Christmas."

Chiles are an excellent source of vitamin C and are additionally rich in vitamins A and E, potassium and folic acid. Chiles are nutritious as well as tasty and do not cause stomach ailments, as is sometimes believed. Initial medical research studies indicate that chiles may have positive effects on heart disease, blood clots and respiratory ailments.

The color of a chile doesn't determine its heat level; that is entirely dependent upon the variety. The pungent heat source in chile peppers is capsaicin, a potent chemical that is not affected by heat or freezing. Capsaicin is found mainly in the white membrane and veins that carry it to the inner walls of the peppers. The seeds absorb some of the heat, but are not the hottest part of the chile. There is a wide range of flavors found in chiles, from cherry to coffee and citrus to pine. In addition to pungency, the textures, flavors and colors of chiles all contribute unique qualities to a dish. Each type of chile has its own personality and can even take on new ones, depending upon how it is prepared.

Eating fiery chiles stimulates the brain to produce endorphins, which create a feeling of stimulation and well-being. Thus, some physiologists theorize that frequent chile-eaters are addicted to chiles and the resulting sensations that are somewhere between pain and pleasure.

Antidotes for Pungency

Dairy products such as milk, sour cream, yogurt or ice cream are the best remedies for relieving "volcanic mouth." Bread, rice, potatoes or flour tortillas will offer some relief by diluting the capsaicin. Beer and wine actually increase heat in the mouth, but are often enjoyed anyway as accompaniments to spicy food.

Selecting Chiles

Fresh chiles should be bright in color, glossy, smooth and firm to the touch. There is no way to tell how hot a chile is by looking at it. One way to check a chile's pungency before using it is to slice off the stem end and lick the flesh attached to it. Select unbroken dried chiles without white spots that have deep color and some flexibility. Ground chile powder should have a rich and spicy aroma and a good strong color.

Storage

For optimum freshness, store fresh chiles in a loosely closed paper bag in the refrigerator for 3 or 4 days. They can also be preserved in a brine solution or pickled. Dried chiles and chile powder maintain their freshness best in airtight containers stored in a cool dark place. Roasted green chiles can be stored in the freezer up to 6 months.

Handling Fresh Chiles

If you are unfamiliar with chiles, it is wise to handle them carefully and wear rubber gloves for chopping and peeling. For some people, chile burns on the skin can cause serious problems. Rinsing your hands first with cooking oil, then washing them with soap and water is an effective method for removing most of the capsaicin. Never touch your eyes, lips, nose or mouth while you are working with chiles.

Roasting and Peeling Fresh Chiles

Many varieties of large green chiles have a tough skin that should be removed before eating. There are several methods for doing this, but the traditional method of roasting is the favorite in Santa Fe. Roasting the chiles removes the skins easily and also produces a wonderful earthy, smoky flavor. The idea is not to fully cook the chile but to quickly blister and blacken the skin. Place fresh chiles on a rack over a gas flame, under a broiler, or on a grill and roast on all sides for 3 to 5 minutes. All of the skin must be blackened or loosened to facilitate peeling, but take care not to over-roast. As the chiles are roasted, place them in a paper or plastic bag to "sweat" until they are cool enough to handle. The skins can then be pulled off or scraped off with a blunt knife, then wiped with a paper towel. Don't rinse the chiles under running water as this dilutes the natural oils and flavors. Peeled chiles can be used immediately or frozen for several months in tightly sealed containers. Roasted chiles can also be frozen unpeeled, which makes them very easy to peel later as the skins tend to separate from the flesh during freezing.

Using Dried Chiles

Remember that dried chiles are just as hazardous to your eyes and skin as fresh ones are. Wear rubber gloves or, after handling, rub your hands with oil, then wash with soap and water. Whatever the intended use, first rinse the chiles lightly, dry with a cloth, then stem and seed. For some recipes, the chiles are then added to the cooking liquid of the dish being prepared. When making either a chile purée or chile powder, the chiles are generally toasted first to deepen their flavors. This is achieved by toasting them lightly for 30 seconds to a minute, or until fragrant, on an ungreased griddle or heavy cast-iron frying pan. They can also be toasted in a 250-degree F oven in a single layer on a baking sheet for 3 to 4 minutes. To make a purée, the toasted chiles are soaked in very hot water for 20 minutes to soften. (Don't use boiling water as it decreases flavor.) The softened chiles are puréed in a blender with a small amount of the soaking liquid and strained to remove any small pieces of skin. To make your own chile powder, grind dry toasted chiles. In place of toasting, some recipes require frying the chiles for a few seconds in hot oil until they puff up slightly. When using any of these methods, take care not to scorch the chiles or they will taste bitter.

Grinding Dried Chiles

First toast as above, then grind dried chiles in small batches in a blender. If a very fine powder is desired, repeat the grinding in small quantities in a spice or coffee grinder. Strain the ground chile powder through a fine mesh strainer.

Commonly Used Chiles in Santa Fe

Dried New Mexico red and fresh New Mexico green chiles are staples in Santa Fe households. Other popular chiles called for in this book are listed below.

Anaheim (mild)

A variety of the New Mexico chile, Anaheims are available almost year-round in supermarkets throughout the country. This very mild chile may be substituted for fresh New Mexico green chiles when less pungency is desired. Their flavor is improved by roasting, which caramelizes some of the natural sugars.

Ancho (mild to slightly hot)

This chile is the heart-shaped, mahogany red-brown dried pod of the poblano measuring about 5 inches long and 3 inches across the shoulder. Sometimes mislabeled as a pasilla, it is available in pod and powdered forms. It is slightly sweet, hinting of plums and raisins with woodsy tones. Anchos are mostly used in sauces, spice rubs, beans, soups and stews.

Cascabel (fairly hot to very hot)

In Spanish, *cascabel* means "rattler," which refers to the rattle of its seeds when the pod is shaken. It is a small round chile, about 1-1/2 inches in diameter. Dark reddish-brown with a smooth skin, cascabels have rich smoky, nutty flavors with tones of tobacco and citrus. This dried chile is most often used in salsas, sauces, soups and stews.

Chipotle (hot to fiery)

A jalapeño that is smoked over hardwood fires to preserve its thick flesh, the chipotle is also known as *chile ahumado* or *chile meco*. Wrinkled, with a dull, mottled tan-brown color and a smoky, sweet flavor, it is available in dried and powder forms, pickled *(en escabeche)* and canned *(en adobo)*. Chipotles are used mainly in beans, soups and sauces.

Habañero (explosive)

The hottest chile in the world, its fierce heat is coupled with tropical fruit tones. Grown mostly in the tropics, this small, lantern-shaped chile ripens to a variety of colors—red, orange, and yellow. Available in fresh and dry forms, it is commonly used in salsas and jerk sauces.

Jalapeño (fairly hot to very hot)

Perhaps the most popular fresh chile in this country, the jalapeño is most often used when bright green in color. It ranges in size from 2 to 3-1/2 inches long and 1/2 to 3/4 inches wide. Its green vegetable flavor complements almost any dish in which chiles are used. Commercially pickled jalapeños *(en escabeche)* are available in cans and jars. There is even a variety of jalapeño for the faint of heart named Jalapeño TAM, which retains its flavor without the heat.

Poblano (mild to fairly hot)

A very dark green fresh chile with a blackish tinge, it is wide at the stem end and tapers to a point. It measures about 4 to 5 inches long and 2 to 3 inches in diameter. Never eaten raw, this chile is roasted and often stuffed, or is made into sauces, soups and stews. Sometimes, it is misnamed in markets as a pasilla.

Serrano (fairly hot to fiery)

A medium bright to dark green chile, the serrano is about the same length as the jalapeño but thinner, measuring about 1/2 inch wide. It is usually eaten in the green mature stage, although it is also available fresh at different levels of ripeness and colors. This chile has a slightly acetic, clean and lively flavor that makes it well suited to fresh salsas and pickled vegetables.

Important Herbs, Spices, Marinades and Seasonings

These ingredients add the robust, complex, and interesting flavors that typify New Mexico's cuisine. The following descriptions are not intended to be a comprehensive list of New Mexico ingredients, but to cover the ones used most frequently in this book.

Achiote Seeds—From the annato tree, achiote is also known as annatto. Brick red achiote paste that has been ground and mixed with spices is often sold in Hispanic markets. It is also available in the hard seed form that requires grinding. Used for coloring and flavoring, its mild and earthy acidic flavor combines well with dried chiles in slow-cooked stews and sauces.

Adobo—A seasoning paste for meats made from ground chiles, herbs and usually containing vinegar, this marinade keeps indefinitely in the refrigerator and adds bright flavors to meats.

Anise Seed—A licorice-flavored spice that was introduced to New Mexico by Spanish settlers, it is used primarily in sweet pastries, notably in biscochitos, New Mexico's state cookie.

Azafran—The Spanish word for "saffron," azafran is the petal of the Mexican orange thistle and is used mainly as a bright color additive, although it does provide a very mild saffron flavor.

Bay Leaf—The leaves from a small tree of the laurel family, bay leaf is used as an herb to be removed after cooking; it imparts a lemon-nutmeg flavor to beans and meat dishes.

Canela—Ceylon cinnamon sticks that are light brown with a shaggy exterior, canela is subtler in flavor than cinnamon and can be used in quantities twice the amount of cinnamon. Its soft surface grinds easily in a coffee or spice grinder and is used in desserts, drinks, and red chile sauces.

Chile Caribe—Coarsely crushed dried red chiles that are used for seasoning. The flavor and heat level depend on the type of chile used.

Chipotles en Adobo—Whole or puréed chipotles are combined with a little ancho chile and seasonings in a flavorful tomato-based sauce. This is one of the few canned products that is highly recommended for cooking.

Cilantro—The most widely used fresh herb in the world, it is used liberally in Santa Fe kitchens as a garnish and a seasoning for savory dishes, marinades and vinaigrettes. There is really no substitute for this leafy herb's distinctive woodsy and grassy flavor. Sometimes called Chinese parsley, it is the green leafy portion of the herb coriander. To maximize freshness, wash a bunch of cilantro and pat dry, cut off the root ends and submerge the stems in a half-filled glass of water. Tent with a plastic bag and refrigerate.

Coriander—Coriander seed comes from the same plant as the cilantro leaf, but its less intense fragrance and flavors of lemon, sage and caraway are quite different. Its best flavor is achieved when the seeds are freshly toasted and ground, then used in dry rubs, pickling, stews, soups, sauces, and bean and corn dishes.

Cumin—Egyptian in origin, cumin came to the Southwest with Spanish settlers. The flavor oils are quite volatile, so toasting and grinding the seeds as needed is recommended. Used in red chile sauces, spice rubs, meats and beans, the spicy nut flavor can be overpowering, so use judiciously.

Epazote—Also known as wormweed, epazote requires cooking to release its flavor. It is primarily used to season beans, dairy-based sauces and sautés of wild greens. The dried leaves are most commonly found in markets, but the fresh herb is occasionally available–use only about a third the amount of dried leaves when substituting it for the fresh. It is also sold in health food stores as a tea that is used for upset stomachs. With a kerosene-like aroma slightly reminiscent of eucalyptus and hints of creosote and anise, there is no comparable substitute. Along with its unique flavor, it is valued for reducing the gaseous qualities of beans.

Marjoram—A member of the mint family, this herb is also known as sweet marjoram and has a taste similar to oregano. Milder and sweeter, it is often used in place of oregano.

Mexican Oregano—After cilantro, this is the second most widely used herb in New Mexico cooking. It is readily available in both fresh and dried forms and is often used interchangeably with marjoram. Dried Mexican oregano contains tiny flower buds that impart a subtle sweetness. Its mild herbaceous flavors complement a variety of foods, including meats, beans, tomatoes, chiles and marinades.

Santa Fe Foodstuffs

These ingredients include some of the food-stuffs that make Santa Fe cooking unique.

Chicos—Chicos are a traditional corn product long used in New Mexico cuisine. Partially shucked ears of corn are roasted for 12 hours in *hornos* (beehive-shaped ovens made of adobe) with ambient heat and a little water. The roasted cobs are removed from the ovens and air-dried until completely dry. The dried kernels are reduced in size, thus the name "chicos," which means "small" in Spanish. Chicos require about 1-1/2 hours of cooking in water or broth to plump up and soften. Their slightly chewy texture adds variety and interest to soups, stews and vegetable dishes.

Corn Husks—Dried corn husks taken from large ears of field corn are traditionally used to prepare tamales and are available at most markets in the Southwest. Choose long wide husks that are not bug-eaten or shredded. In season, fresh corn husks can be used. Carefully remove the husks by cutting them off at the base and peeling off one at a time. Select the larger ones for using as wrappers. If you intend to use them at a later date, layer the leaves in stacks of 10, and loosely roll up each stack lengthwise. Seal in a plastic storage bag and freeze up to 6 months. Thaw the husks in warm water and pat dry before using.

Frijoles—In Santa Fe, this Spanish term usually refers to pinto beans. *Frijoles refritos* is the Spanish name for "refried beans." Mild-flavored pinto beans are well suited to the stronger flavors of aromatic herbs and toasted spices. *Frijoles negros,* or black beans, have a hearty, slightly smoky flavor and are used in soups, sauces and side dishes. Cooked and canned beans should be rinsed and well drained prior to adding to salsas.

Jicama—Sometimes labeled in markets as a Mexican potato, this legume grows underground as a tuber. A bulbous root vegetable, it has a light brown thin skin, white crisp flesh and a sweet nutty flavor. It is usually eaten raw in salads or as an appetizer with dips.

Masa Harina—In Spanish, the term means "dough flour" and refers to the coarse flour made from ground dried corn kernels. Tortillas are made from finely ground masa harina, and tamales from the coarser grind. The term *masa* refers to the corn dough that is used to make tortillas, tamales and other dishes. In the Southwest, freshly prepared masa is available in supermarkets.

Pepitas—The word pepitas refers to hulled seeds from several varieties of large squash and pumpkins. Large unshelled pumpkin seeds and shelled smaller green seeds can be found in supermarkets. Pepitas have a relatively low fat content and may be substituted for piñons and pecans. They are used in salads and salsas and to thicken and flavor red and green Mexican sauces called pipians.

Piñon Nuts—*Piñon* is the Spanish word for "pine"; piñon nuts are the seeds from the cones of several varieties of pine trees. Harvesting them is labor-intensive since the shelling is usually done by hand. They are used in sweet and savory dishes and are ground to thicken sauces and pestos.

Posole—White or yellow corn kernels are boiled with slaked lime and water to remove their hulls, then rinsed and dried. The kernels are ground into masa harina for tamales or corn tortillas, or used whole and cooked to soften. The starchy side dish bears the same name as the posole corn from which the dish is made. Dried as well as partially cooked frozen posole is available in most Southwest markets. It is often stewed with pork, red chile pods and other spices.

Roma Tomatoes—Flavorful Roma, or plum, tomatoes are especially well suited to southwestern dishes that require roasted or dried tomatoes. Small and pear-shaped, they have a high ratio of flesh to seeds and juice, making them the perfect tomato for salsas. Do not refrigerate as chilling reduces their flavor.

Tomatillos—Sometimes known as Mexican green tomatoes, they are not actually tomatoes but a fruit that is a member of the nightshade family and closely related to the gooseberry. Resembling a small bright-green tomato with a papery husk, they have a sticky residue on their skin that requires washing to remove. Tomatillos, which are used in cooked sauces or raw in salsas and dips, have an apple-lemon-herb flavor that is further deepened and developed by roasting.

Santa Fe Cuisine

Whether you are eating in restaurants or private homes, these descriptions will be helpful in familiarizing yourself with the local cuisine.

Biscochito—New Mexico's official state cookie, a biscochito is a type of sugar cookie–shortbread traditionally made with lard and flavored with anise.

Burrito—A flour tortilla wrapped around a warm filling such as meats, chicken, potatoes or beans, and garnished with a variety of salsas, cheese, and lettuce.

Cajeta—A thick, rich and tangy Mexican caramel sauce, cajeta will keep indefinitely in the refrigerator. Traditionally made from equal parts of goat's and cow's milk, it can be made entirely from cow's milk for a slightly different flavor. Cajeta is found in jars in Hispanic markets.

Calabacita—The Spanish word for "squash," it also refers to a vegetable side dish of zucchini, yellow squash, onions, green chiles and sometimes cream or cheese.

Capirotada—Raisins, nuts and other dried fruits are often added to this very sweet traditional bread pudding made with a rich caramel sauce and cheese instead of eggs and cream.

Carne Adovada, or Carne Adobada—A spicy, red-chile-flavored meat dish, this is generally made with pork that has been marinated overnight in a thick chile sauce and then simmered slowly in the oven until tender.

Carnitas—Marinated strips of meat sautéed with onions and chiles that are usually served wrapped in a flour tortilla.

Chile Relleno—A large roasted and peeled chile, usually stuffed with cheese, is dipped in a light batter and deep-fried. Baked versions are becoming increasingly popular.

Chorizo—This Mexican sausage, traditionally made from fresh pork, is highly seasoned with red chile powder, garlic and other spices. It is often mixed with scrambled eggs and used as a breakfast burrito filling.

Empañadas—Small turnovers filled with sweet or savory fillings that are baked or deep fried.

Enchiladas—Stacked or rolled soft corn tortillas that are filled with meats, chicken, seafood, vegetables, cheese, and red or green chile sauces. A favorite breakfast dish in Santa Fe is cheese and red chile enchiladas topped with a fried egg.

Flauta—Spanish for the word "flute," a flauta is a corn tortilla wrapped around a savory filling, rolled into a cylinder and deep fried. It is usually served with a garnish of lettuce, salsa, sour cream or guacamole.

Natillas—Similar to the classic French floating island dessert, traditional natillas are composed of a silky custard topped with clouds of uncooked meringue. Contemporary recipes include variations for poaching the meringue or substituting whipped cream.

Salsa—Spanish for "sauce," it usually refers to a chunky or smooth cool vegetable sauce served as a dip or as a topping for a variety of dishes.

Tamale—A filling of meat, chile, vegetable or fruit is encased in masa dough, wrapped in individual softened corn-husk packets and steamed. There are many contemporary twists to this traditional food, but the classic pork tamale remains the favorite for many Santa Feans.

Tortillas—Thin, unleavened round breads made from either corn or wheat flour and cooked quickly on an ungreased griddle. A tortilla is eaten as bread or served either crisp or soft and wrapped around various meat, bean, or vegetable fillings. In New Mexico, flour tortillas tend to be relatively thick and are best eaten when fresh. (See the following information and recipes for making tortillas.)

Tostada—Sometimes referred to as a "Mexican pizza," this crisply fried or baked tortilla is topped with beans, meat, or any variety of fillings, and often garnished with cheese, lettuce, tomatoes, and salsa.

Making Corn and Flour Tortillas

Ethnic breads seem to change very little over the years. The corn tortillas made here today are probably very similar to those originally brought by the Mexicans to New Mexico. The early Spanish settlers in Santa Fe did not adapt readily to unleavened corn tortillas. So, preferring wheat breads, they brought in wheat seeds from Spain and the northern state of Sonora, Mexico. Wheat was grown in the mid-1800s in the Taos area and supplied flour for the newly favored wheat tortillas. Today both types of tortillas are used in humble as well as sophisticated dishes.

Tortillas are especially delicious when freshly made and eaten while the air is still fragrant with their earthy aroma. Tortillas tend to dry out and stiffen when they are not well wrapped and kept warm after cooking. Look for tortilla warmers and baskets that are especially made for this purpose.

Corn Tortillas

Yield: 12 tortillas
2 cups masa harina
1/2 teaspoon salt
1 cup plus 2 tablespoons warm water

Mix the masa harina with the salt in a mixing bowl. Add the warm water and stir with a wooden spoon until the dough holds together in a ball. Knead a few times, adding a little extra water or masa harina if the dough seems too wet or dry. (It should feel pliable, not crumbly.) Wrap the dough well in plastic wrap and let it stand 30 minutes to 1 hour. Heat an ungreased heavy griddle or cast-iron skillet over medium-high heat. Divide the dough into 12 pieces, roll into balls and cover with a damp cloth. Press the balls of dough on a tortilla press, flattening to about 1/16 inch thick between 2 sheets of plastic cut from heavy plastic bags. Peel off the top layer of plastic and invert the tortilla onto your hand. Remove the remaining piece of plastic and lay the tortilla on the preheated griddle. Cook for 1 minute, or until lightly speckled. Turn the tortilla over and cook 30 seconds, pressing down on the tortilla with a spatula. Repeat with the remaining balls of dough. As they are cooked, stack the tortillas in an unsealed plastic bag and cover with a towel to keep warm.

Note: With a little practice, you can use two small wooden cutting boards in place of a tortilla press to press the balls of dough. Place one board on a sturdy surface, lay a piece of plastic on it, and place a ball of dough in the center. Cover with the other piece of plastic, and then press down hard with the second board to form a 1/16-inch-thick tortilla. Peel off the plastic and cook as above. Repeat the process with the remaining balls of dough.

Blue Corn Tortillas

With their deep earthy flavor and slate gray-blue color, blue corn tortillas are a specialty of northern New Mexico. These tortillas are more difficult to make than yellow corn tortillas because the dough is more fragile and dry. Blue corn meal produces a somewhat stiff tortilla that is generally used for flat enchiladas or as breads, chips or tostadas.

Yield: 14 to 16 tortillas
1 cup masa harina
1 cup blue corn meal
Pinch of salt
1-1/8 cups of water

Mix the masa harina, blue corn meal and salt together in a bowl. Add the water and stir well with a fork. Knead the dough until it holds together; it will be a little crumbly. Proceed by following the steps described above in the recipe for Corn Tortillas, beginning with resting the dough 30 minutes.

Note: Since blue corn tortillas do not puff as well as yellow corn tortillas, some tortilla makers use 2 ungreased cast-iron frying pans or griddles to cook the tortillas (or 1 large griddle over 2 burners). The tortilla is cooked on the first pan, which has been preheated to medium heat, for 40 seconds, or until edges begin to dry. Next, the uncooked side of the tortilla is placed on the second pan, which has been pre-heated to medium-high, and cooked about 50 seconds; it is turned again and cooked 10 to 20 seconds. This method produces the lightest blue corn tortillas.

Fluffy Flour Tortillas

Yield: 8 to 10 six-inch tortillas
2 cups unbleached white flour
1 tablespoon baking powder
1 teaspoon salt
1/4 cup vegetable shortening or lard
3/4 to 1 cup warm water

Mix the dry ingredients together in a bowl. Cut the shortening in with a pastry blender or two knives until the mixture resembles a coarse meal. Add 3/4 cup water and stir with a fork until the dough comes together. Turn the dough out on a lightly floured surface and knead 12 times. The dough should be soft but not sticky. Add extra flour or warm water, a teaspoon at a time, to adjust the consistency. Wrap well with plastic wrap and let rest 30 to 40 minutes.

Divide the dough into 8 to 10 portions and flatten slightly with your hand into 4-inch round discs on a lightly floured surface. Cover with plastic and let rest 10 more minutes.

Heat a large cast-iron skillet or griddle over medium-high heat. Using a flour-dusted rolling pin, roll out a disc until you have a flat 6-inch circular tortilla of uniform thickness. Roll from the center of the disc back and forth, giving it a quarter turn after each roll. Avoid rolling off the edges of the circle of dough as this makes the edges of the cooked tortilla brittle. The dough will be springy, but if it is too rubbery to work with, cover and allow it to rest for a few minutes and start on another disc.

Roll out 3 or 4 at a time, then cook. Transfer a tortilla to the skillet, taking care not to stretch it. Cook for about 20 to 30 seconds, then turn and cook about 15 seconds on the other side. Flour tortillas should be cooked quickly, just until lightly browned and speckled. If the tortillas puff up, flatten with a spatula. As the tortillas are cooked, place them in an unsealed plastic bag and cover with a towel.

Note: Flour tortillas are best when eaten very fresh as they lose their tenderness when refrigerated more than 2 days or frozen.

Techniques for Getting Started

Some of these fundamental techniques have been used in daily food preparation for hundreds of years. Others combine hand-made authenticity with timesaving contemporary procedures.

Quick-Soaking Beans

Cooking dried beans, particularly at higher altitudes, can sometimes take 3 or more hours. Soaking overnight is the usual method for pre-softening beans, but that means you must plan ahead. This quick-soak method replaces overnight soaking. Place cleaned beans in a large pot with enough water to cover by several inches. Bring to a boil over medium heat and boil 1 minute. Remove pot from the heat, cover and let stand 1 hour. Drain and rinse the beans, return to the pot and add water again to cover by several inches. Cook according to your recipe.

Cleaning Nopales

Wear gloves until you get the hang of working with nopales (vegetable-like cactus pads from the prickly pear). First, trim off the edges around the outside of the cactus paddle. Using the tip of a sharp knife, cut out the spiny thorns and little nodes around the base of the thorns on both sides.

Dry-Roasting Corn

Heat a seasoned cast-iron skillet or heavy sauté pan over high heat and add enough fresh (or defrosted and drained frozen) corn kernels to cover the bottom 2 or 3 kernels deep. Allow the corn to sizzle and brown around the edges before turning. The corn will turn a dark brown as it caramelizes, adding a wonderful flavor.

Frying Fresh Corn Tortillas for Chips

When moist fresh tortillas are fried, they will make greasy chips. On the other hand, if they are too dry they will be very crunchy. Dry the fresh tortillas on a clean surface for about 1 hour to reach the proper leathery stage before frying.

Roasting Tomatoes, Tomatillos, Onions and Garlic

These vegetables are all roasted by using the same easy method–roasting on a baking sheet under a preheated broiler. Prepare the vegetable(s) that you are using as follows: halve the tomatoes; halve cleaned and husked tomatillos; peel and slice the onions; separate the garlic cloves and brush with a little vegetable oil. Arrange one or more of the vegetables cut side down on the baking sheet. Broil tomatoes, tomatillos and onions, turning once, until they are blackened. Broil garlic to a golden brown and peel when cool. Watch carefully as the goal is to blacken the vegetables, not to turn them into charcoal. Be sure to add any accumulated juices from the pan to the dish you are preparing. Many cooks like to incorporate the blackened skins of the tomatoes and tomatillos into salsas.

Peeling Tomatoes

Cut a small X at the stem end of the tomatoes. Place tomatoes in a pot of boiling water, and blanch for 15 seconds. (Leave less ripe tomatoes in the water for 30 seconds.) Drain tomatoes in a colander and place in a bowl of ice water. Pull the skins off using the tip of a small sharp knife. Peaches and apricots can be peeled in the same manner.

Roasting Bell Peppers

See the method described for roasting fresh green chiles on page 13.

Toasting and Grinding Whole Spices

The flavors of cumin, coriander and dried herbs such as Mexican oregano are awakened when they are freshly toasted and ground. In a dry sauté pan over medium-high heat, place a single layer of herbs or spices. Stir constantly as they begin to darken and release their fragrance. Remove to a plate when they have toasted uniformly, usually about 1 minute. Watch carefully as herbs and spices burn quite easily. Grind in a spice or coffee grinder or with a mortar and pestle to the desired texture.

Toasting Nuts and Seeds

Toasting will enhance the flavor of all nuts and seeds. Large nuts can be toasted on a baking sheet in a 350-degree F oven, whereas smaller nuts are easily handled in a dry skillet on top of the stove. The cooking time will depend upon the freshness of the nuts.

Washing Fresh Greens

Fill a large bowl or sink with very cold water, add the greens and soak a few minutes. Carefully lift the leaves out and shake off the excess water. Any sand and grit will remain at the bottom.

Helpful Equipment

Today there are many timesaving devices that duplicate age-old labor-intensive techniques for grinding, puréeing, shredding and chopping. The recipes in this book can be completed with a basic set of cookware in a standard kitchen, including such items as a blender, electric mixer and food processor. In addition, the following specialized pieces of cooking equipment would be useful to have on hand:

Cast-iron skillet or griddle
Deep-fat thermometer
Instant-read meat thermometer
Mandoline (a manual piece of equipment that has adjustable blades; used to slice or shred vegetables)
Mortar and pestle
Plastic squeeze bottles
Spice and coffee grinders
Steamer (for tamales)
Stovetop grill rack
Tortilla press

Mail-order and local sources for southwestern ingredients, goods and equipment are listed on page 144.

Artistic Appetizers and Intimate Buffets

A Palette of Salsas on Canyon Road

Pineapple-Chipotle Salsa • Dilled Green Chiles • Screaming Hot Habañero Salsa • Tomatillo Guacamole • Crunchy

Garden Vegetable Salsa • Roasted-Corn and Olive Salsa • Plantain Chips • Traditional Blue or Yellow Corn

Tortilla Chips • Baked Corn or Flour Tortilla Chips • Southwest Pita Crisps • Red Chile Potato Chips

A Collection of Museum-Quality Morsels

Seasoned Seed and Mixed-Nut Jumble • Cumin- and Coriander-Spiced Black Olives • Herb-Marinated

Green Olives with Jalapeños • Goat Cheese Mini-Cheesecakes in Pecan Crusts

A Gallery Cocktail Buffet

"Make Your Own" Steak Taquitos • Pickled Peppers and Summer

Vegetables • Shrimp Ceviche in Cucumber Cups • New Mexico Green Chile Tart

A Post-Show Party

Duck, Shiitake and Gouda Quesadillas with Peach and Red Pepper Salsa • Jalapeño-Marinated

Shrimp with Olives and Cherry Tomatoes • Crudites with Dry Chile Dunk and

Seasoned Citrus Salt • Picadillo Empañadas

Santa Fe is a visual-arts haven. Museums and galleries abound, sculptures decorate the landscape, and murals cover many adobe walls. And, of course, there is the world-renowned Canyon Road. Long before becoming the artistic center of Santa Fe, the Canyon Road area was comprised of a few scattered houses, pastures and farmland. Now, the historic 1.2-mile stretch of road is lined with galleries, studios, private homes, craft and jewelry shops, magnificent gardens and restaurants.

Much of the city's social scene revolves around the art world. The transition from sleepy little town to international art center began slowly in Victorian times when Englishman Fred Harvey built his hotels and eateries along the railway lines in the West. In an effort to make the area a destination point for tourists, Harvey helped commercialize the traditional arts of Native Americans–pottery, textiles, crafts and jewelry–to add that key element–shopping–to the activity mix.

Soon, travelers were collecting traditional decorative arts of the Spanish as well. They appreciated religious objects such as *retablos* (saints painted on wood), crosses, and carvings of saints and the Holy Family for their beauty and spiritual significance.

In the mid-nineteenth century, the first government census of the Pueblo Indians was conducted, and Peter Moran, an expedition artist, recorded them in their traditional dress, sharing the beauty and history of these ancient cultures with the world at large. In the 1920s, a group of artists called Los Cinco Pintores established the first art colony in Santa Fe; by the end of that decade, painter Georgia O'Keeffe arrived from the East Coast and later helped to immortalize the northern New Mexico landscape. The scenery and the dazzling quality of light continues to draw artists and galleries to this day.

As artists fell in love with the sculpted mesas, the piñon-covered mountains and the stark river valleys of the area, locals fell in love with the artists. For years, Santa Fe has been recognized as the third-largest art market in the country.

Many Canyon Road galleries welcome the public on Friday evenings for opening-night receptions. It's a tradition among locals to attend these occasions, meet the artists, sip cocktails and sample some creative appetizers. In the summer months, the sun sets around eight so there is ample time for strolling and shopping before giving serious thought to dinner.

The downtown area also has its share of excellent galleries that add to the social scene with festive, catered, opening-night cocktail parties. The superb museums near the Plaza–notably the Georgia O'Keeffe Museum, Palace of the Governors, the Museum of Fine Arts and the Institute of American Indian Arts Museum–will broaden your perspective of Santa Fe and its people historically, culturally and artistically.

Yet to fully appreciate Santa Fe is to explore the artful flavors of the region. Get started with the following recipes!

A Palette of Salsas on Canyon Road

Salsas, various blends of chopped, diced or puréed fruits or vegetables accented with fresh herbs, heighten the flavors of any meal. They can spice up or cool down the palate. Cooked or raw, salsas also add colorful visual appeal to foods. They are served as dips, toppings for eggs, meats, poultry and fish, and as condiments for quesadillas, tacos, nachos and burritos.

Pineapple-Chipotle Salsa
Sweet and smoky flavors characterize this sensational salsa.

Yield: about 3-1/2 cups

1 medium pineapple, peeled and cored
2 teaspoons olive oil
1/2 cup diced red onion
2 cloves garlic, minced
2 tablespoons brown sugar
2 tablespoons cider vinegar
2 tablespoons freshly squeezed lime juice
1/4 cup canned chipotles en adobo (or to taste), chopped (see p. 18)
2 tablespoons finely chopped cilantro
1 teaspoon coarsely ground salt

Coarsely chop pineapple and transfer to a colander set over a bowl; drain about 5 minutes. Reserve 3 tablespoons pineapple juice.

Heat oil in a large skillet over medium-high heat. Add pineapple and onion; sauté until lightly browned. Add garlic and sauté 1 minute. Transfer pineapple mixture to a bowl. Reduce heat to medium and add brown sugar, cider vinegar, lime juice, and reserved pineapple juice to the skillet. Cook 2 minutes, stirring occasionally; allow to cool slightly, then pour over pineapple and stir in remaining ingredients. Cover and refrigerate up to 3 hours before serving.

Dilled Green Chiles
The assertive heat of the chiles is balanced by the sweetness of the sugar. In addition to being delicious, this dish is rich in vitamin C. Serve it with crackers or salted tortilla chips.

Yield: about 3 cups

1/2 cup vinegar
1/2 cup sugar
1 clove garlic, finely minced
2 teaspoons chopped fresh dill weed (or 1 teaspoon dried dill)
1/2 teaspoon mustard seed
1/2 teaspoon salt
3 cups fresh hot New Mexico green chiles, roasted, peeled and chopped (or thawed and well-drained frozen chiles)*

Mix together all ingredients except chiles in a small saucepan and place over medium heat. Simmer 3 minutes, stirring occasionally. Cool to room temperature before adding green chiles. Refrigerate up to 24 hours. Drain before serving.

About 5 roasted long green chiles produce 1 cup chopped chiles.

Screaming Hot Habañero Salsa

The hottest chile in the world, the habañero has fruity undertones. A touch of orange juice cuts the heat some-what and adds a fresh citrus flavor.

Yield: about 1-1/4 cups

8 habañero chiles, stemmed and chopped (or 12 serrano or jalapeño chiles for less heat)
2 serrano chiles, stemmed and chopped
1/2 cup freshly squeezed orange juice
1/4 cup chopped red onion
2 cloves garlic, minced
2 teaspoons minced flat-leaf parsley

Mix all ingredients together in a bowl and refrigerate until serving time.

Tomatillo Guacamole

Tomatillos look like small green tomatoes, but they are actually part of the gooseberry family. When used raw, tomatillos taste like a mixture of lemon, plum and apples. Cooking brings out a tart flavor that is easily balanced with a little sugar. Guacamole is best when served immediately.

Yield: about 3 cups

12 tomatillos, husked, rinsed, and roughly chopped (or well-drained canned tomatillos)
3 jalapeño chiles, roughly chopped
2 cloves garlic, chopped
1 or more teaspoons sugar (depends on acidity)
1-1/2 teaspoons salt
1/4 cup lime juice

3 ripe avocados, peeled, pitted, and roughly chopped
6 scallions, finely chopped
1/4 cup fresh cilantro leaves

Place tomatillos, jalapeños, garlic, sugar, salt and lime juice in the bowl of a food processor and pulse until smooth. Add avocados and pulse again until mixture is just blended. Pour into a bowl and stir in scallions and cilantro. Taste and adjust seasonings. If not serving immediately, cover surface of gua-camole with plastic wrap and refrigerate up to 2 days.

Crunchy Garden Vegetable Salsa

Of the many versions of tomato-vegetable salsas, this is a favorite because of its garden-fresh medley of chopped vegetables.

Yield: 3 cups

6 large Roma tomatoes
1/2 medium cucumber, peeled and seeded
1/2 medium red onion
1/2 red bell pepper, seeded
1/2 green bell pepper, seeded
3 jalapeño chiles, seeded
1 tablespoon minced fresh cilantro leaves
1-1/2 teaspoons dried Mexican oregano
1 tablespoon minced Italian parsley
1 tablespoon extra virgin olive oil
2 tablespoons sherry vinegar
1/2 teaspoon salt

Cut tomatoes, cucumber, onion, red and green bell pepper, and jalapeño chiles into uniform 1/4-inch dice. Combine with remaining ingredients in a bowl. Refrigerate at least 1 hour to allow flavors to develop. Drain any accumulated juice before serving.

Roasted-Corn and Olive Salsa

With its earthy flavor, this salsa is more than a dip. Serve on bruschetta, or roll it in a flour tortilla for a tasty treat.

Yield: about 2-1/4 cups

2 cups fresh or frozen corn kernels
1/2 cup sliced black olives
1/2 cup diced red pepper
2 tablespoons diced jalapeño chiles
1/4 cup diced red onion
2 teaspoons minced garlic
1 teaspoon chopped fresh oregano
    (or 1/2 teaspoon dried oregano)
1/4 cup olive oil
2 tablespoons fresh lime juice
1 tablespoon white wine vinegar
Salt and pepper to taste
1/4 cup toasted and chopped blanched almonds

Place corn in a heavy dry skillet over medium-high heat. Roast about 10 minutes, or until corn is lightly browned, stirring frequently. Allow to cool, then combine with remaining ingredients except almonds. Refrigerate up to 8 hours; sprinkle with almonds just before serving.

Plantain Chips

Plantains (starchy cooking bananas with green skins) are a South American staple and, when fried, offer an interesting alternative to corn chips.

Yield: 8 servings

1 tablespoon chile caribe (see p. 18)*
1 tablespoon coarse salt
2 teaspoons finely grated orange peel
6 cups canola or peanut oil
4 green plantains

Stir chile caribe, salt and orange peel together in a small bowl. Heat oil in a large pot or deep-fryer to 375 degrees F. Peel plantains and slice into long thin strips with a mandoline or vegetable peeler. (This method produces curled loops of plantain chips as they are fried.) Fry in batches until golden and crisp; remove with a slotted spoon and drain on baking sheets lined with paper towels. Sprinkle with salt mixture while still hot.

*Chile caribe can be omitted for a less-pungent flavor.

Traditional Blue or Yellow Corn Tortilla Chips

These chips have an unbeatable fresh flavor and crunch that you don't find in commercially prepared chips, which often have numerous additives and preservatives. They are easy to make and easier to eat!

Blue or yellow corn tortillas
Vegetable oil
Salt (optional)
Lime juice (optional)
Chile powder (optional)

To prepare fresh corn tortillas for frying, see pages 23–24.

Stack any number of tortillas; cut into desired shapes—strips or wedges—with a sharp knife. Heat 1 to 2 quarts vegetable oil in a deep fryer or large pot to 350 degrees F. Fry tortillas in batches about 1 minute, or until crisp and golden. Remove with a slotted spoon and drain on paper towels. Sprinkle with salt, lime juice or chile powder. Store in a cool, dry place up to 3 days.

CHEF'S CORNER: *The seasoning for Red Chile Potato Chips also makes a delicious sprinkle for oven-roasted potato wedges.*

Baked Corn or Flour Tortilla Chips

This healthier version of the traditionally fried chip has a wonderful nutty flavor.

Cut tortillas in the same manner as for fried chips. Preheat oven to 400 degrees F. Arrange tortilla pieces in a single layer on a large baking sheet that has been coated with vegetable oil. Spray pieces lightly with vegetable oil and season with salt. Bake, turning once, approximately 10 minutes, or until golden. Store in a cool, dry place up to 3 days.

Note: Making your own chips is a good way to use tortillas that have begun to dry out. For special shapes, use cookie cutters.

Southwest Pita Crisps

Middle East meets Southwest in a crisp with character.

Yield: 48 crisps

1/4 cup olive oil
2 teaspoons dried Mexican oregano
1/2 teaspoon freshly toasted and ground cumin
1 teaspoon coarse salt
6 large pockets of whole wheat pita bread

Preheat oven to 450 degrees F. In a large bowl, combine all ingredients except pita bread. Stack pita bread and cut into eighths. Add pita pieces and toss to coat well. Spread pita pieces in a single layer on 2 lightly oiled baking sheets. Bake 5 minutes, turn pita pieces over with tongs, and continue baking another 4 minutes, or until golden and crisp. Let cool completely, then store up to 2 days in an airtight container. If necessary to re-crisp, pita chips can be baked in a 400-degree F oven 2 to 3 minutes.

Note: Make crunchy baked sesame-coated pita or tortilla crisps by brushing one side of tortilla pieces or pita wedges with beaten egg whites and coating with sesame seeds. Place on a lightly oiled baking sheet and bake at 350 degrees F until lightly browned, about 8 minutes.

Red Chile Potato Chips

Homemade chips are an irresistible treat. Serve these chips warm; when thoroughly cooled, they can be stored in an airtight container up to 1 week.

Yield: 3 cups

Using a mandoline or food processor, cut 2 large peeled raw sweet potatoes or white potatoes into very thin slices. Soak sliced potatoes in ice water 5 minutes. (Can be prepared ahead up to 4 hours and held in ice water until cooking.) Drain well and place in single layer on heavy kitchen towels. Pat dry. Fill a heavy pot half full of vegetable oil and heat to 350 degrees F. Fry potatoes in batches until nicely browned. Using a slotted spoon, transfer chips to trays lined with paper towels to drain. While still warm, sprinkle with red chile seasoning.

Note: Use this same method to make chips with other root vegetables (carrots, beets, celery root, parsnips).

Red Chile Seasoning (enough for 1 pound of potatoes):
1 teaspoon red chile powder (any variety)
1/2 teaspoon salt
1/2 teaspoon sugar
1/2 teaspoon cayenne chile powder (optional)

Mix all ingredients together in a small bowl.

A Collection of Museum-Quality Morsels

With more than a dozen museums in Santa Fe, you're bound to find a few that will capture your interest. The art, architecture and history of Santa Fe are well represented by these world-class institutions. After viewing all these artistic and cultural treasures, enjoy the following artful edibles with a cool cocktail.

Seasoned Seed and Mixed-Nut Jumble

Seeds, nuts and spices are combined for an updated version of traditional mixed nuts.

Yield: about 6 cups

3 cups shelled pepitas (see p. 20)
3 tablespoons soy sauce
1 cup macadamia nuts
1 tablespoon ancho chile powder
1/2 teaspoon freshly toasted and ground cumin seed
2 tablespoons olive oil, divided
1 cup raw pistachios
1 teaspoon freshly toasted and ground coriander seed
2 teaspoons coarse salt
1 cup whole blanched almonds or pecan halves

Place pepitos and soy sauce in a small bowl and toss until mixed. Place on a baking sheet and toast in a 400-degree F oven 10 minutes, or until lightly browned. In a small bowl, toss macadamias with ancho chile powder, ground cumin and 1 tablespoon olive oil. Spread on a baking sheet and toast in a 400-degree F oven about 5 minutes, until lightly browned. Toss together pistachios, coriander and remaining oil and salt; spread on a baking sheet. Toast in 400-degree F oven about 5 minutes, until lightly browned. Place toasted nuts on paper towels to absorb excess oil. When cool, combine all nuts in a large bowl and mix together. If a more piquant flavor is desired, add some cayenne pepper to final nut mixture.

Note: Nuts may require some stirring during toasting to prevent burning and sticking.

Cumin- and Coriander-Spiced Black Olives

Olives are great for impromptu snacking or as a light hors d'oeuvre with cocktails or wine. They keep about three months when refrigerated. Black and green olives can be mixed after marinating separately.

Yield: 2 cups

2 cups oil-cured black olives
1/4 cup olive oil
2 teaspoons whole cumin seed, toasted
2 teaspoons whole coriander seed, toasted
1 teaspoon anise seed, toasted
2 teaspoons fennel seed
1/2 teaspoon freshly ground black pepper
2 tablespoons orange-juice concentrate

2 tablespoons fresh lemon juice
4 cloves garlic, peeled and cut into thin slivers
Pinch of ground cinnamon
Pinch of ground nutmeg

Place olives in a container with a secure lid. Mix remaining ingredients in a small bowl. Pour over olives and toss to combine. Store in refrigerator at least 4 days before serving, shaking container daily. Bring olives to room temperature before serving.

Herb-Marinated Green Olives with Jalapeños

Rosemary and thyme add an herbal contrast to these spicy olives. For the best flavor, serve at room temperature.

Yield: about 2 cups

2 cups large green Spanish olives, lightly crushed
1/4 cup sliced jalapeño or serrano chiles
4 cloves garlic, peeled and crushed
1 tablespoon olive oil
1 tablespoon cider vinegar
1/2 teaspoon freshly toasted and ground cumin
1/2 teaspoon dried Mexican oregano
1/4 teaspoon crushed rosemary
1/2 teaspoon dried thyme
2 bay leaves

Drain liquid from olives and rinse. Place olives and chiles in a container in which they will just fit. Whisk remaining ingredients together and pour over olives and chiles. Stir well and marinate at room temperature at least 1 day; stir olives occasionally. They will keep for a month in the refrigerator.

Goat Cheese Mini-Cheesecakes in Pecan Crusts

Santa Feans are blessed with a local variety of high-quality fresh goat cheeses. The mellow flavor of goat cheese is sparked in this recipe with flecks of sweet sun-dried tomatoes and hot cayenne pepper. Serve these cheesecakes warm or at room temperature.

Yield: 3 dozen

1 cup fresh whole-wheat bread crumbs
1 cup finely ground pecans
2 tablespoons melted butter
1/2 teaspoon salt
8 ounces cream cheese, softened
10 ounces soft goat cheese
2 tablespoons finely chopped, oil-packed, sun-dried tomatoes, well drained
2 large eggs, beaten lightly
1 teaspoon cayenne pepper (or to taste)
2 tablespoons chopped fresh herbs (basil, thyme, rosemary, oregano, chives, parsley, tarragon)
Sprigs of fresh herbs

Preheat oven to 350 degrees F and lightly spray three dozen nonstick, 1/8-cup mini-muffin cups with vegetable oil. Place bread crumbs, ground pecans, butter and salt in a medium bowl and mix until combined. Spoon a heaping teaspoon of crumb mixture into each muffin cup; with fingers, press mixture into bottoms and sides of cups. Bake shells 5 minutes. Place cream cheese and goat cheese in the bowl of an electric mixer and beat until light and fluffy. Add eggs, pepper and herbs; beat until well combined. Divide cheese mixture between shells. Bake until puffed, about 12 to 15 minutes. Allow to cool 5 minutes on rack before unmolding. Garnish each cheesecake with a sprig of fresh herbs.

A Gallery Cocktail Buffet

This buffet typifies the type of fare served by Santa Fe galleries at their gala openings. Generally, openings take place on Friday evenings, providing a social and festive start to summer weekends. For a casual party, serve just the taquitos and pickled vegetables with Mexican beer. For a more elaborate affair, add the other appetizers and serve with margaritas, sangria, or a New Mexico wine.

"Make Your Own" Steak Taquitos

Guests enjoy building their own custom taquitos, or "little tacos." There is nothing more appealing than fragrant, warm corn tortillas filled with fresh-tasting crunchy salsa and tender, juicy bites of steak.

Yield: 24 taquitos

Salsa:
2-1/2 cups chopped Roma tomatoes
1 cup chopped white onions
1/2 cup chopped fresh cilantro
1 teaspoon chopped fresh oregano
**   (or 1/2 teaspoon dried oregano)**
5 tablespoons fresh lime juice
2 jalapeño or serrano chiles, seeded and chopped
Salt to taste

Combine all ingredients in a medium bowl. Cover and chill up to 4 hours before serving.

Tortillas:
24 (4-inch) corn tortillas (if small corn tortillas are unavailable, use a cookie cutter to cut larger ones to size)

Preheat oven to 350 degrees F. Wrap tortillas in heavy foil and heat in oven 15 minutes.

Steak:
2 pounds skirt steak, well-trimmed
Garlic salt
Pepper
2 cups crumbled queso fresco or mild feta cheese

Prepare barbecue or preheat broiler. Season steak generously with garlic salt and pepper. Grill or broil steak to desired doneness. Allow to sit 5 minutes before slicing thinly across the grain and cutting into bite-sized pieces. Place meat on a platter; arrange bowls of salsa, queso fresco and corn tortillas for guests to assemble their own taquitos.

CHEF'S CORNER: *Keep tortillas warm and moist by wrapping them in several layers of cloth tea towels.*

Pickled Peppers and Summer Vegetables

Large jars of these pickled vegetables are often served as bar snacks in Mexico. They will add a spicy dimension to any appetizer platter or entrée.

Yield: about 5 cups

1-1/2 cups white wine vinegar

2 cups water

1 teaspoon sugar

1 pound cauliflower, trimmed and sliced into bite-sized pieces

1 pound thin green beans, ends snipped (steam briefly if beans are tough)

1 large red onion, halved lengthwise and cut into thin slices

2 carrots, peeled and cut into matchstick-sized pieces

1 red bell pepper, seeded and cut into thin slices

8 jalapeño chiles, stemmed, seeded and sliced

1 tablespoon chopped fresh herbs (oregano, thyme, sage or marjoram)

2 tablespoons olive oil

Coarse salt and freshly ground black pepper to taste

Bring vinegar, water and sugar to a boil in a noncorrosive pan. Place cauliflower in a large glass or stainless-steel bowl and pour vinegar mixture over it. Allow to stand while preparing other vegetables.

Add remaining vegetables to cauliflower and sprinkle with herbs, oil, salt and pepper. Cover and marinate vegetables at room temperature 3 hours. Refrigerate at least 1 day before using; bring to room temperature before serving. Pickled vegetables will keep several weeks in the refrigerator.

Shrimp Ceviche in Cucumber Cups

The acidity of the limes complements the bold flavor of the shrimp, giving this dish its bright taste. Ceviche is commonly served with saltine crackers or tortilla chips. It also makes an excellent first course served on endive leaves or on a bed of shredded lettuce with large tostada chips.

Yield: about 24 servings

Shrimp Ceviche:

1 pound medium green (uncooked) shrimp, peeled, deveined and coarsely chopped

4 small limes

1/2 cup diced red onion

2 jalapeño chiles, stemmed, seeded and chopped

2 tablespoons chopped cilantro

2 teaspoons chopped parsley

Salt and freshly ground pepper

1/3 cup plus 1 teaspoon extra virgin olive oil

2 Hass avocados

2 Roma tomatoes, cored and diced

2 garlic cloves, finely minced

Place shrimp in a single layer in large glass pan. Squeeze juice of 3 limes over shrimp and scatter onion, jalapeños, cilantro and parsley on top. Season lightly with salt and pepper. Drizzle olive oil over shrimp and stir to combine. Cover and marinate in refrigerator at least 4 hours, stirring occasionally.

Sauté garlic in 1 teaspoon olive oil until golden. Just before serving, peel and pit avocados and cut into small dice. Toss with juice of remaining lime. Add tomatoes and garlic to avocado and stir lightly into shrimp. Fill Cucumber Cups with Shrimp Ceviche up to 1 hour before serving.

Cucumber Cups:

4 large cucumbers, peeled and cut into 3/4-inch-thick slices

Using a melon-baller or tip of a small spoon, scoop out seeds and enlarge seed core. (Take care not to cut through the bottoms of the cucumber cups.) Place upside down on trays lined with paper towels to drain until ready to use.

New Mexico Green Chile Tart

Pungent green chiles provide a sharp counterpoint to the rich blend of cheeses in this tart. It is perfect for cocktail parties as well as luncheons and informal suppers.

Yield: 16 thin wedges

Tart Shell:

2 cups flour

1/2 teaspoon salt

3 tablespoons chilled unsalted butter, cut into 1/4-inch pieces

1/2 cup chilled vegetable shortening

3 to 4 tablespoons ice water

1 egg, lightly beaten

CHEF'S CORNER: *Did you know that green shrimp marinated in lime juice "cooks" without heat, giving the shrimp a firm, flavorful texture?*

Mix flour and salt in a food processor fitted with a steel blade. Scatter pieces of butter over flour and process with several one-second pulses. Add shortening in pieces and process until mixture resembles coarse cornmeal. Gradually add just enough water for dough to come together. Form into a flat disk, dust lightly with flour and wrap in plastic. Chill at least 30 minutes or overnight.

Preheat oven to 425 degrees F. Let dough warm up at room temperature about 10 minutes. On a lightly floured board, roll dough out to fit in a 10-inch tart pan with a 1/2-inch overlap. Place dough in pan and tuck overhanging dough under to form a rim. Line shell with waxed paper or parchment and fill with beans or metal pie weights to prevent shell from puffing up and shrinking. Place shell in oven and bake 10 minutes. Remove paper and weights, brush bottom and sides with egg, and continue baking until crust is pale gold, another 2 to 5 minutes. Reduce oven temperature to 350 degrees F.

Filling:
2 tablespoons butter
3 scallions with green tops, sliced
1 teaspoon minced garlic
1-1/2 cups heavy cream
4 large egg yolks, lightly beaten
1 cup shredded Monterey Jack cheese
1 cup shredded sharp cheddar cheese
1/2 teaspoon salt
3/4 cup roasted, peeled and chopped hot
**   New Mexico green chiles**
**   (or well-drained frozen chiles)**
1 teaspoon chopped fresh oregano
**   (or 1/2 teaspoon dried Mexican oregano)**
1/2 teaspoon toasted and ground coriander seed
2 tablespoons coarsely chopped cilantro

Heat butter in a small skillet. Add scallions and garlic; sauté briefly until garlic has softened. Let cool. Combine scallions and garlic with remaining ingredients and stir until well mixed. Pour mixture into baked tart shell. Place on baking sheet and bake 35 minutes, or until filling is set and lightly browned. Serve warm or at room temperature.

A Post-Show Party

These menu choices provide food as inspired as the artists' creations. Table settings are often works of art utilizing unique locally crafted ceramics and glassware for a picture-perfect post-show party.

Duck, Shiitake and Gouda Quesadillas with Peach and Red Pepper Salsa

The richness of the duck is contrasted by the fruity salsa in this imaginative blend of flavors and textures. These quesadillas also make a delicious light luncheon entrée.

Yield: six 8-inch quesadillas (36 wedges)

Duck:
1 whole 1- to 1-1/2-pound boneless duck breast with skin, halved
1 teaspoon vegetable oil

Preheat oven to 350 degrees F. Trim duck breasts of excess skin and fat. Prick skin all over with a fork without piercing meat. Heat a heavy skillet over moderately high heat until hot, then add oil. Season duck with salt and pepper and place skin side down in skillet. Reduce heat to medium and cook until skin is golden, about 3 minutes. Turn duck over and cook 3 minutes more. Remove duck from skillet and place in a small roasting pan. Roast in preheated oven about 5 or 6 minutes, or until an instant-read thermometer inserted in the thickest part of the meat reads 165 degrees F. Allow duck to cool, discard skin and hand-shred the meat. Refrigerate until ready to use.

Barbecue Sauce:
2 tablespoons olive oil
1/2 cup chopped red onion
1 tablespoon minced garlic
5 Roma tomatoes, chopped

1/2 cup ketchup
3 tablespoons dark molasses
2 tablespoons dark brown sugar
1 tablespoon honey
1 tablespoon ancho chile powder
1 teaspoon cayenne
1/4 cup red wine vinegar
1/4 cup water
1 tablespoon Worcestershire sauce
Salt and pepper to taste

Sauté onion in olive oil over medium heat until softened. Add garlic and sauté 1 minute. Place onions, garlic and remaining ingredients in a medium saucepan and simmer on low heat 20 minutes, stirring occasionally. Cool 5 minutes, then purée in a blender. Add enough sauce to liberally moisten duck meat.

Note: There will be some sauce left over for making additional quesadillas or for using as a barbecue sauce with other grilled meats or poultry.

Mushroom and Cheese Mixture:
6 shiitake mushrooms, cleaned and sliced
1 tablespoon olive oil
1/4 pound Gouda cheese, shredded
1/4 pound Monterey Jack cheese, shredded
2 teaspoons chopped cilantro

Sauté mushrooms in olive oil over medium heat until soft. When mushrooms have cooled, stir in cheeses and cilantro.

Note: The barbecue sauce, duck and mushroom-cheese mixtures can be prepared a day ahead for easy last-minute assembly.

Peach and Red Pepper Salsa (about 2 cups):
3 ripe peaches, peeled and diced
1/2 cup diced red pepper
2 tablespoons diced jalapeño
2 tablespoons finely diced red onion
1 teaspoon minced garlic
1 tablespoon chopped cilantro
1/2 teaspoon toasted and ground cumin seed
2 tablespoons red wine vinegar
1 tablespoon orange-juice concentrate
1 tablespoon freshly squeezed lime juice
1 tablespoon extra virgin olive oil
Salt to taste

Toss all ingredients together in a large bowl. Cover and refrigerate up to 3 hours.

Note: Mangoes or papayas make an excellent substitute for peaches.

Assembly:
12 (8-inch) flour tortillas
Olive oil
Chile powder

Preheat oven to 400 degrees F. Place 6 tortillas on a sheet pan and spread with duck and mushroom-cheese mixture. Top with remaining 6 tortillas; press down lightly. Brush tops of quesadillas with olive oil and sprinkle lightly with chile powder. Bake 5 to 10 minutes, or until lightly browned and cheese has begun to melt. Slice each quesadilla into 6 pieces and top with dollops of Peach and Red Pepper Salsa.

Jalapeño-Marinated Shrimp with Olives and Cherry Tomatoes

Jalapeños add bright notes of flavor to this colorful Southwest alternative to shrimp cocktails. Olives and cherry tomatoes add color to the fiesta of flavors.

Yield: 20 servings

3 pounds large shrimp in shells
8 cups water
1 large seafood-seasoning boil bag
1 lemon, quartered
1 tablespoon chopped fresh Italian parsley
2 bay leaves
1 tablespoon salt
1/2 teaspoon paprika
1/4 cup tarragon wine vinegar
1/2 cup white wine vinegar
1 cup extra virgin olive oil
2 cloves garlic, crushed
1 teaspoon cayenne pepper
1 (16-ounce) can pitted whole black olives, drained
1 (8-ounce) can pickled jalapeño peppers, drained
2 cups small whole cherry tomatoes

Place water, seafood-seasoning bag, lemon, parsley, bay leaves and salt in a large pot and bring to a boil. Add shrimp, reduce to a simmer, and continue simmering an additional 3 minutes. Pour into a colander and rinse immediately with ice water. When cooled, drain, peel and devein shrimp.

Whisk paprika, vinegars, oil, garlic and pepper together. Place shrimp, olives and jalapeños in a large glass bowl and combine with oil and vinegar mixture. Marinate overnight, stirring occasionally. Stir in tomatoes and drain well before serving with toothpicks.

Crudites with Dry Chile Dunk and Seasoned Citrus Salt

These simple and healthy appetizers are fat-free and taste great! The dunk and the salt also make yummy sprinkles for fresh vegetables or a sensational seasoning for grilled fish or chicken breasts.

Crudites:
Raw carrots, celery, jicama, other favorite
vegetable dippers

Trim, peel and cut vegetables into uniform sticks. For convenience, prepare vegetables a day before serving, cover with ice-cold water and refrigerate. Drain and shake off excess water before serving.

Dry Chile Dunk (about 3/4 cup):
2 tablespoons sugar
1 teaspoon ground sage
1/2 cup red chile powder (mild, medium, or hot)
1 teaspoon ground cumin
1/2 teaspoon ground coriander
1/2 teaspoon ground canela (or 1/4 teaspoon cinnamon)
Coarse salt to taste

Combine ingredients in a spice mill or coffee grinder. Whir until all ingredients are ground into fine powder. Pour mixture into a small, heavy nonstick skillet. Stir constantly over low heat about 3 minutes, or until spices slightly darken in color. Lower heat if necessary to avoid scorching. Pour on a plate to cool before placing in a jar to store at room temperature.

Seasoned Citrus Salt (about 1/2 cup):
1/2 cup coarse salt
Grated rinds of 1 orange, 1 lemon and 1 lime
1 teaspoon finely minced fresh oregano
1 teaspoon finely minced fresh mint

Mix all ingredients together in a small bowl. Serve in a large-holed shaker as a tasty sprinkle for crunchy fresh vegetables.

Note: Fill a basket with green-and-white vegetables for an attractive presentation.

Picadillo Empañadas

Empañadas are mini-turnovers that contain either sweet or savory fillings. In these tasty empañadas, raisins provide a sweet contrast to the woodsy cumin and coriander. Traditionally deep-fried in lard, today's empañadas are often baked instead.

Yield: about 24

Pastry*:
1-1/2 cups all-purpose flour
1 cup masa harina
1 teaspoon baking powder
1 teaspoon salt
1/2 cup unsalted butter, melted and cooled
1/2 cup plus 1 tablespoon water
2 large eggs

Preheat oven to 375 degrees F. Spray 2 baking sheets with vegetable oil. Mix flour, masa harina, baking powder and salt in a large bowl. Stir in melted butter. Stir water and 1 egg together in a small bowl and add to flour mixture. Knead in the bowl until a smooth and pliable dough is formed.

Working with half the dough at a time, roll out on a floured surface to 1/8 inch thickness, then cut out rounds using a 3-inch cookie cutter. Re-roll scraps and cut additional rounds. Whisk remaining egg in a small bowl until blended. Place 1 tablespoon of filling in center of each round. Lightly brush edges with egg and fold dough over; press edges with a fork to seal. Place on prepared baking sheets and brush tops with beaten egg. Bake until light brown, about 20 minutes.

*Note: This pastry can be made the previous day. Wrap well with plastic wrap and refrigerate until needed. Allow pastry to soften slightly before rolling.

Filling**:
1 tablespoon olive oil
12 ounces of lean meat (pork tenderloin, leg of lamb, or beef sirloin), well trimmed and cut into 1/4-inch cubes

1 tablespoon chile powder
1 teaspoon freshly toasted and ground coriander
1/2 teaspoon freshly toasted and ground cumin
1-1/2 teaspoons cinnamon
1 teaspoon ground allspice
1/8 teaspoon ground cloves
2 tablespoons raisins, soaked and drained
1/4 cup tomato sauce
1/4 cup chicken broth or water
6 tablespoons chopped toasted almonds
Salt and pepper to taste

Heat oil in a large skillet over medium-high heat. Add meat, chile powder, coriander, cumin, cinnamon, allspice and cloves to skillet. Stir-fry about 4 minutes. Add raisins, tomato sauce and broth; simmer until most of the liquid evaporates. Remove from heat and mix in almonds. Season with salt and pepper and cool to room temperature before filling pastry rounds.

**Note: This filling can be made and refrigerated 2 days before using.

Farmers' Market Favorites

A Trio of Local Delights

Creamy Chilled Corn Soup • Goat Cheese Flans on Crisp Baby Greens

with Tangy Tomato Vinaigrette • Peach Right-Side-Up Cake

A Farmers' Market Brunch

Squash Blossom Frittata with Crunchy Tomato-Radish Salsa • Cornmeal Bacon Scones with

Fresh Herb Butter • Crisp Potato-Veggie Hash • Pineapple, Papaya and Raspberries with Lime-Rum Syrup

A Farmers' Market Celebration

Golden Gazpacho with Basil Croutons • Grilled Sea Bass Fillets Wrapped in Corn Husks, with

Minted Cucumber Salsa • Black Bean, Corn and Arugula Salad with Balsamic Cumin

Vinaigrette • Frozen Honey Mousse with Red Berry Sauce and Toasted Almonds

A Garden-Fresh Supper

Farmers' Market Tortilla-Chicken Soup • Sweet Roasted Red Beet Salad • Santa Fe

Gingerbread with Tangy Poached Apricots

The Farmers' Market is a summer highlight here in Santa Fe. Held in the historic Railroad Yard on Tuesday and Saturday mornings, Farmers' Market features the very best of the region's fresh and organic produce.

The atmosphere of the marketplace is relaxed and rural, with bales of hay set up in the shade to accommodate weary shoppers. The vendors' tables are neatly organized in rows with the fruits and vegetables arranged in heaps or baskets. Some farmers sell their produce right out of the backs of their cars or trucks. Locals roam the aisles with cups of coffee, talking with friends and tasting samples. Some shoppers have basketsful of freshly baked goodies hooked over one arm while others cradle one perfect plant in their palms. Children nibble on fruit and wave at the Santa Fe and Southern train as it chugs along the tracks past the market on its way to Lamy.

The city's top chefs can often be seen at the market, squeezing and prodding the produce and planning their menus according to what looks best. You sometimes see their public trying to wheedle recipes from them. Add a variety of impromptu performances by local dancers and musicians and you have a Santa Fe happening.

Today, there are about 150 farms in northern New Mexico, many of them tended by the same families for generations. Considering the area's dry climate and sandy, loamy soil, the local farmers produce an amazing variety of offerings all summer long.

In June, the first of the spring crops come to market. Pinto beans, snow and sugar-snap peas, spinach and acres of broccoli are displayed alongside onions and cabbages. Beets, turnips and other root vegetables are harvested out of the sun-warmed soil. Sweet and sour cherries are the first fruit of the season, making it a popular month in town for fresh cherry pies and tarts.

By July, the market takes on the warm scents of sun-ripened apricots; eggplant and cucumbers make their seasonal debut, as do summer squashes in an array of colors, shapes and textures. Carrots, green beans and herbs such as dill and fennel come to market. Apples, peaches, nectarines and fresh herbs form the basis of the condiments, sauces and spreads that are available for sampling.

In August, green chile is harvested. Hundreds of pounds of chiles are roasted at the market, and their sweet, sharp scent blankets the city. Shoppers stand knee deep in truckloads of fresh corn, searching for the perfect ear. Cantaloupe and honeydew melons, bushels of pears and boxes of fresh-picked tomatoes and potatoes crowd the narrow rows of the market in Santa Fe's most productive growing month.

Many towns throughout the U.S. hold farmers' markets, but few are as colorful and spirited as Santa Fe's. So, do as the locals do and enjoy a taste of Farmers' Market favorites.

A Trio of Local Delights

This simple summer menu is served chilled for a cool midday meal. It features some of the area's favorites—corn, goat cheese, organic greens, tomatoes and peaches—all of which are produced by local farmers and sold at Farmers' Market. Add a warm loaf of crusty bread to round out the meal.

Creamy Chilled Corn Soup

Corn is a New Mexico staple that has long held great cultural, religious and dietary significance for Native Americans of the Southwest. The soup's pretty orange hue comes from azafran, a spice whose flavor is similar to that of the more costly saffron.

Yield: 8 servings

3 tablespoons butter
2 leeks, white part only, sliced
1 tablespoon chopped shallots
2 teaspoons mild chile powder
1 teaspoon azafran (or 1/4 teaspoon saffron)
5 cups fresh yellow corn kernels (about 8 ears)
4 cups chicken broth

1/2 teaspoon freshly toasted and ground coriander
1 cup unsweetened coconut milk
  (or low-fat coconut milk)
Salt and white pepper to taste
2 tablespoons coarsely chopped cilantro

Melt butter in a soup pot over medium heat. Add leeks and shallots, cover and sweat until soft, about 5 minutes. Add chile powder and cook, stirring, 1 minute. Add azafran, corn, broth and coriander. Simmer uncovered 20 minutes. Add coconut milk and allow to cool slightly. Pour three-fourths of the soup into a blender and purée until smooth. Combine purée and reserved soup. Refrigerate until well chilled. Season to taste with salt and pepper. Serve soup garnished with chopped cilantro.

Note: For an interesting variation, add 1/4 cup cooked and puréed carrots to the completed soup mixture.

Goat Cheese Flans on Crisp Baby Greens with Tangy Tomato Vinaigrette

Many years ago a goat could be found in almost every yard in Santa Fe. Local women made mild-flavored goat cheese on a daily basis and incorporated it into a variety of dishes. Crisp fresh greens provide contrast for the delicate flavor and texture of Goat Cheese Flans.

Yield: 8 servings

Goat Cheese Flans:
1-3/4 cups heavy cream
1/2 cup fresh mild goat cheese, room temperature
5 large egg yolks, slightly beaten
1 tablespoon minced fresh chives
1/2 teaspoon salt
1/2 teaspoon freshly ground black pepper

Heat oven to 300 degrees F. Lightly butter eight 3/4-cup ramekins. Place all ingredients in the bowl of an electric mixer and mix on low speed until well combined. Spoon mixture into ramekins. Set them in a baking dish and add hot water to reach halfway up the sides of the ramekins. Bake about 30 minutes, or until tops are lightly browned. Transfer to a wire rack to cool 5 minutes. Serve cold or at room temperature.

Note: The flans can also be baked in a single buttered soufflé dish, increasing the baking time from about 30 minutes to 40 to 50 minutes.

Tangy Tomato Vinaigrette:
1 pound Roma tomatoes, cored and cut into fourths
1 teaspoon salt
2 teaspoons Dijon mustard
1 tablespoon sherry wine vinegar
2 teaspoons finely chopped fresh oregano
1 teaspoon finely chopped fresh thyme
1/4 cup extra virgin olive oil
1 tablespoon finely chopped chives

Place tomatoes in blender or food processor and purée until smooth. Pour into a small bowl and add remaining ingredients. Whisk until well combined.

Crisp Baby Greens:
8 ounces mixed salad greens
12 red and yellow cherry tomatoes, halved
12 long chives

To serve: Toss salad greens and tomatoes with Tangy Tomato Vinaigrette and arrange on individual salad plates. Unmold flans on top of greens and garnish with chives.

Peach Right-Side-Up Cake

European settlers brought fruit trees to the area and they have flourished here ever since. Make this buttery rich cake when sweet peaches are abundant in the summer.

Yield: 8 servings

4 cups sliced fresh peaches
1 cup sugar, divided
1/4 cup unsalted butter
2 eggs
1/2 teaspoon almond extract
1 cup plus 2 tablespoons sifted all-purpose flour
1 teaspoon baking powder
1/4 teaspoon salt
1 teaspoon canela (or 1/2 teaspoon cinnamon)
Cinnamon-flavored whipped cream

Preheat oven to 350 degrees F. Butter and flour the bottom of an 8-inch square pan. Sprinkle peaches with 1/2 cup sugar and let stand 30 minutes. Using an electric mixer, cream butter and 1/2 cup sugar until light. Beat in eggs one at a time, then add almond extract. Whisk together flour, baking powder and salt in a small bowl. Mix in creamed butter by hand until well combined. Spread batter over bottom of prepared pan.

Drain peaches, reserving syrup; distribute peaches on top of batter. Combine 2 tablespoons flour and 1 teaspoon canela with reserved syrup; pour over peaches. (If peaches are tart, sprinkle with 2 tablespoons sugar.) Bake 45 to 50 minutes, or until deep golden brown. Serve warm with whipped cream.

A Farmers' Market Brunch

A popular custom among many Santa Feans is to rise with the sun in order to arrive for the market's early opening, select choice produce, and then transform it into a gourmet brunch for friends and family. Weekend brunches are a summer tradition for social Santa Feans.

Squash Blossom Frittata with Crunchy Tomato-Radish Salsa

Early in the summer, squash plants produce beautiful yellow blossoms that have long been considered a delicacy by native peoples. The flowers must be picked first thing in the morning before the blossoms open and used the same day. The crunchy salsa pairs perfectly with the tender frittata.

Yield: 6 servings

Stuffed Squash Blossoms:
4 ounces goat cheese or cream cheese
1/2 cup grated Parmesan cheese
1 egg
2 teaspoons chopped fresh basil
1 teaspoon chopped fresh epazote
**   (or 1/2 teaspoon dried epazote)**
2 teaspoons chopped fresh oregano
2 teaspoons chopped fresh parsley
Salt and pepper to taste
12 to 14 squash blossoms
2 eggs, beaten
1/2 cup flour
2 tablespoons butter

Combine cheeses, egg, fresh herbs, salt and pepper. Wash each squash blossom and snip off the long green stems of the "male" blossoms; pat dry with paper towels. Open each flower and fill with 1 tablespoon cheese mixture, carefully stuffing it down around the stamen. The stuffed blossoms can be refrigerated up to 2 hours before sautéing.

Melt butter in a large skillet over medium-high heat. Dip each blossom in beaten eggs, roll in flour and shake off excess before placing in skillet. Sauté until golden, turning once. Drain on paper towels.

Egg Mixture:
7 large eggs
2 tablespoons milk
Salt and pepper to taste
2 tablespoons vegetable oil or clarified butter

Beat eggs, milk and seasonings together until smooth. Warm a large, ovenproof nonstick skillet over medium heat. Add oil or butter to the pan and heat. Arrange stuffed squash blossoms in skillet and pour egg mixture over them.

Reduce heat to medium-low and cook 30 seconds. Using a pancake turner, lift edges of the frittata so that the uncooked eggs run off and underneath the cooked portion. Continue lifting until there are no more uncooked eggs, then place under broiler 30 to 60 seconds to finish cooking top. Loosen the frittata around its edges with a spatula and slide onto a plate. Cut into wedges and serve with Crunchy Tomato-Radish Salsa.

Note: Warming the empty pan before adding oil helps prevent eggs from sticking to the pan.

Crunchy Tomato-Radish Salsa (2 cups):
1/4 cup minced red onion
3 tablespoons fresh orange juice
2 tablespoons fresh lime juice
1 cup chopped Roma tomatoes
1/4 cup diced red radish
2 serrano chiles, minced (or jalapeños for less heat)
1/4 cup coarsely chopped cilantro
Salt to taste

Place all ingredients in a small bowl and stir gently to combine. The salsa can be made up to 2 hours ahead.

Cornmeal Bacon Scones with Fresh Herb Butter

These hearty scones are loaded with character. The essence of fresh herbs is preserved in this flavorful butter, which will also enhance breads, muffins, mashed potatoes and a variety of vegetables.

Yield: 9 servings
Cornmeal Bacon Scones:
1-1/4 cups all-purpose flour
1/2 cup yellow cornmeal
2 tablespoons sugar
2 teaspoons baking powder
1/2 teaspoon baking soda
1/4 teaspoon salt
1/4 cup butter, chilled and cut into small pieces
4 slices bacon, cooked, drained and chopped

2/3 cup buttermilk
2 eggs, lightly beaten

Combine first 6 ingredients in a bowl. Cut in butter with a pastry blender or 2 knives until mixture resembles peas; stir in bacon. Combine buttermilk and eggs; add to dry ingredients, stirring just until dry ingredients are moistened. With floured hands, pat dough into a 9-inch square on a baking sheet that has been sprayed with vegetable oil or lined with parchment paper. Using a sharp knife, score deeply into 9 squares. Bake 20 minutes, or until golden. Serve warm with Fresh Herb Butter.

Note: A good local raspberry jam is extraordinary with these scones, making for a delicious sweet-salty flavor combo.

Fresh Herb Butter (about 1-1/3 cups):
1 cup flat-leaf parsley leaves, loosely packed
1/4 cup snipped fresh chives
1 clove garlic, minced
2 teaspoons fresh thyme leaves
2 teaspoons fresh rosemary leaves
2 teaspoons fresh tarragon leaves
2 sticks unsalted butter, room temperature
2 teaspoons fresh lemon juice
Salt and white pepper to taste

Wash and dry parsley well. Place parsley, chives, garlic, thyme, rosemary and tarragon in the bowl of a food processor fitted with a steel blade. Pulse 10 to 12 times, stopping to scrape down sides, until herbs are coarsely chopped. Add butter, lemon juice and seasonings; mix well, taking care not to overmix. Taste and adjust seasonings. Transfer to a sealable container, or roll with plastic wrap into a log. Refrigerate up to 1 week.

Crisp Potato-Veggie Hash

This crispy potato dish is loaded with Farmers' Market vegetables, making it a seasonal favorite. Simple herb seasoning allows the freshness of the vegetables to shine through.

Yield: 6 to 8 servings

1-1/4 pounds small red potatoes, cut into 1/2-inch cubes

4 carrots, peeled and cut into 1/2-inch cubes

1 tablespoon butter

1 tablespoon olive oil

1 red pepper, cut into 1/2-inch cubes

1 yellow pepper, cut into 1/2-inch cubes

1/2 pound asparagus tips

4 scallions, green and white parts, thinly sliced

1 teaspoon chopped fresh thyme

1 tablespoon chopped fresh cilantro

1 tablespoon chopped fresh parsley

Salt and pepper to taste

Cook potatoes and carrots in separate saucepans in boiling water until crisp-tender. Drain and set aside. In a large non-stick skillet, heat butter and oil over medium heat. Add peppers, sauté and stir until crisp-tender, about 10 minutes. Add asparagus and scallions; continue to sauté another 2 minutes. Add potatoes, carrots, thyme, cilantro and parsley; mix with sautéed vegetables. Season with salt and pepper. Cook over medium heat about 10 to 15 minutes, stirring occasionally, until a golden crust forms on potatoes.

Pineapple, Papaya and Raspberries with Lime-Rum Syrup

This Mexican-influenced dessert is sweet and simple. It provides a colorful and lively tropical finish to any meal.

Yield: 6 servings

1 pineapple (about 1-1/2 pounds), peeled and cored

1 papaya (about 1-3/4 pounds), peeled and seeded

1 cup raspberries

1 lime, washed well and cut crosswise into paper-thin slices

1/4 cup corn syrup

1/4 cup fresh lime juice

1 teaspoon chile powder

2 tablespoons rum or orange juice

1/2 teaspoon pure vanilla extract

Cut pineapple and papaya crosswise into slices and arrange on a serving platter. Scatter raspberries around edge of platter.

In a small pan over medium heat, stir lime slices, corn syrup, lime juice and chile powder until boiling; simmer on low heat 1 minute. Allow to cool slightly, then stir in rum and vanilla. Spoon syrup and lime slices over fruit.

A Farmers' Market Celebration

Exploring the market with friends is one way to begin celebrating a leisurely weekend, Santa Fe style. Locals plan their menus around the herbs, fruits and vegetables that are at their very best. There's nothing more fun than meandering through the rows while shopping for produce, then sharing in the creation of a lovely meal with friends.

Golden Gazpacho with Basil Croutons

Gazpacho, a traditional Spanish cold vegetable soup, is featured here in a contemporary version that is as healthful as it is colorful. Crisp basil-flecked croutons top this summertime favorite.

Yield: 6 servings

Golden Gazpacho:
4 cups yellow cherry tomatoes
2 cloves garlic, minced
1/2 cup coarsely chopped cilantro
1 cup chopped red bell pepper, divided
1 cup chopped yellow bell pepper, divided
1/2 cup diced red onion, divided
1 cup peeled, seeded and chopped cucumber
2 jalapeño chiles, seeded and chopped
1/2 cup diced jicama
1/2 cup seasoned rice wine vinegar
1/2 cup tomato juice
2 tablespoons olive oil
2 teaspoons chopped fresh oregano
2 teaspoons coarse salt
1/2 teaspoon freshly ground pepper

In a blender or food processor, purée tomatoes, garlic, cilantro, 1/2 cup each of red and yellow bell peppers, and 1/4 cup of onion. Transfer purée to a bowl and stir in remaining ingredients. Cover and chill gazpacho at least 2 hours. Serve topped with Basil Croutons.

Basil Croutons:
3/4 cup packed fresh basil leaves, washed and well dried
1/4 cup extra virgin olive oil
1/2 teaspoon salt
1/2 teaspoon pepper
3 cups firm bread, crusts trimmed, cut into 1/2-inch cubes

In a blender or food processor, purée basil, oil, salt and pepper until smooth. Preheat oven to 350 degrees F. Place bread cubes on a lightly oiled baking sheet and toss with enough basil oil to coat liberally. Stirring occasionally, bake croutons 10 to 15 minutes, or until crisp and golden brown. Extra croutons may be used for other soup or salad creations.

Variation: Serve gazpacho in large margarita glasses in which a few tablespoons of tomato juice have been frozen. Top with cooked shrimp instead of croutons, or chop shrimp and stir into gazpacho.

Grilled Sea Bass Fillets Wrapped in Corn Husks, with Minted Cucumber Salsa

For centuries, southwesterners have enjoyed foods cooked in corn husks, which impart an earthy flavor and seal in moisture. The Minted Cucumber Salsa adds a refreshing note to the rich flavor of the fish.

Yield: 6 servings

6 (4- to 6-ounce) skinless fillets of sea bass, halibut, red snapper, or salmon

Marinade:
6 tablespoons olive oil
3 tablespoons fresh lime juice
2 teaspoons chopped fresh cilantro
2 tablespoons chopped white onion
Salt and pepper to taste

Combine all marinade ingredients in a small bowl. Place fish in a shallow pan and brush marinade over both sides of the fish. Marinate 20 minutes, then drain and pat dry.

Preparing corn husks: Carefully remove husks from 6 large ears of unshucked corn, reserving the largest outer husks—about 24—for wrapping fish. Tear 12 narrow lengthwise strips from remaining husks to tie corn-husk packages. Cut kernels from corn cobs and reserve for Black Bean, Corn and Arugula Salad.

Assembling fish packets: Place 2 corn husks smooth side up on a work surface and overlap them on longer sides by 2 inches. Center a third husk on top of the other two for reinforcement. Place a piece of fish in center of corn husks. Fold sides of corn husks over fish to cover completely. Tie both ends with a corn-husk strip. (If husks are small, use 4 husks to enclose fish.) Repeat with remaining fish to make 6 packets.

Grilling corn-husk packets: Preheat grill to medium-high. Lightly brush corn-husk packets with water if dry; arrange around the edges on the grill to avoid burning over hottest part of the coals. Grill about 6 minutes on each side, turning once, or until husks are slightly charred and fish is cooked through. Serve each fish packet with a small cup of Minted Cucumber Salsa.

Minted Cucumber Salsa (about 2 cups):
2 cups peeled, seeded and diced cucumber
1/4 cup minced red onion
1/4 cup chopped fresh mint
2 teaspoons chopped fresh cilantro
3 tablespoons apple cider vinegar
1 tablespoon extra virgin olive oil
1-1/2 tablespoons honey
Salt and pepper to taste

Combine all ingredients in a medium bowl and stir gently to blend. Taste and adjust seasonings. This salsa can be made 2 hours ahead.

Black Bean, Corn and Arugula Salad with Balsamic Cumin Vinaigrette

This hearty high-fiber salad pairs two of the region's best-loved staples with the slightly bitter bite of arugula.

Yield: 6 servings

Salad:
1-1/2 cups cooked black beans, rinsed
1-1/2 cups corn kernels, reserved (cook until crisp-tender if large)
3 Roma tomatoes, halved and diced
6 cups arugula, torn into bite-sized pieces
Shaved Parmesan cheese

Place all ingredients in a large salad bowl and toss with enough Balsamic Cumin Vinaigrette to coat well. Garnish each serving with shaved Parmesan cheese (use a vegetable peeler for this task).

Balsamic Cumin Vinaigrette:
1/2 cup olive oil
1/4 cup balsamic vinegar
1/2 teaspoon toasted and ground cumin seed
2 large cloves of garlic, minced
3 tablespoons chopped fresh basil
1 teaspoon minced fresh rosemary
Salt and pepper to taste

Whisk all ingredients in a small bowl until well blended. Adjust seasonings as needed.

**CAUTION: *Do not make any recipe that calls for uncooked eggs if salmonella is present in these products in your area.*

**NOTE: *Pasteurized egg substitutes may be used in some recipes.*

Frozen Honey Mousse with Red Berry Sauce and Toasted Almonds

Early Spanish settlers observed the Pueblo Indians gathering and eating wild honey and soon incorporated it in their diets. This mousse's smooth texture and subtle flavor comes alive with the addition of sweet-tart Red Berry Sauce topped with crunchy Toasted Almonds.

Yield: 8 servings
Frozen Honey Mousse:
1 cup whipping cream
6 egg yolks, room temperature**
1/2 cup honey (lavender honey is a good choice)
1 teaspoon pure vanilla extract
1/2 teaspoon ground canela
      (or 1/4 teaspoon ground cinnamon)

Whip cream until stiff. In an electric mixer bowl, beat egg yolks until frothy. Add honey, vanilla and canela; beat 5 to 8 minutes, or until thick and pale. Fold in whipped cream.

Line a loaf pan with plastic wrap that extends beyond top of pan. Pour mousse into prepared pan, wrap well, and freeze at least 6 hours, preferably overnight. Unmold frozen mousse, peel off plastic wrap and cut into thin slices.

Red Berry Sauce:
12 ounces fresh or frozen unsweetened berries
      (blackberries, red raspberries, or strawberries)
Sugar to taste

If using frozen berries, defrost and drain. Purée berries and sugar in a blender or food processor until smooth. Strain purée, using a rubber spatula to push sauce through a fine mesh strainer. Refrigerate up to 2 days.

Toasted Almonds:
1/2 cup sliced almonds

Stir almonds constantly in a nonstick skillet over medium heat until lightly toasted. Set aside to cool.

To serve, spoon Red Berry Sauce on each dessert plate and place slices of mousse on top. Garnish with almonds.

Note: The mousse is easy to prepare and may be kept, well wrapped, in the freezer up to 2 weeks. The sauce can be made ahead 2 days and refrigerated.

A Garden-Fresh Supper

A garden-fresh soup, a robust salad, and a dessert crowned with luscious local fruit make an excellent choice for a relaxed summer supper. Do as the locals do and enjoy this repast outside under the shade of a portal or later under the stars.

Farmers' Market Tortilla-Chicken Soup

This soup offers a contemporary take on a classic recipe. It is chock-full of healthy vegetables that will warm body and soul on cool summer evenings.

Yield: 12 or more servings

Tortilla-Chicken Soup:

1/4 cup olive oil

2 cups chopped onion

1 tablespoon minced garlic

1 tablespoon chile powder (mild, medium, or hot)

3 cups Roma tomatoes, roasted, peeled and chopped (see p. 26)

2 teaspoons dried Mexican oregano (or 1 teaspoon fresh Mexican oregano)

1-1/2 teaspoons toasted and ground cumin seed

12 cups chicken broth

2 cups grated carrots

1 cup roasted, peeled and cubed red bell pepper (see pp. 26, 13)

2 cups roasted, peeled and chopped New Mexico green chiles (see p. 13)

1-1/2 cups sliced zucchini

1-1/2 cups sliced yellow squash

1 (1-pound) chicken breast, cooked and cut into 1/2-inch strips

1/2 pound pork or beef chorizo, sautéed and well drained (optional)

Salt and pepper to taste

Heat oil in a large pot over medium-high heat, add onion and sauté until golden. Add garlic and sauté 1 minute. Stir in chile powder and sauté 1 minute. Add tomatoes, oregano and cumin; simmer until slightly thickened, about 5 minutes. Add chicken broth, carrots, red pepper, chiles, zucchini, yellow squash, chicken strips, and chorizo. Simmer about 10 minutes, or until vegetables are done. Season with salt and pepper.

strips in a single layer on prepared sheet. Bake until crisp, turning once, about 10 minutes. Combine cilantro, lime peel, lime juice and garlic in a small bowl. Serve bowls of soup topped with tortilla strips, cilantro mixture and cheese.

Note: Warm flour tortillas or crusty olive bread are good accompaniments to the soup. Offer slices of juicy ripe watermelon for a quick refreshing dessert.

Sweet Roasted Red Beet Salad

Beets have a high sugar content, so roasting them concentrates their flavor to an intense, slightly caramelized sweetness. Their vibrant purple-red color and deep flavor make a bold contrast to the fresh lively flavors of the soup.

Yield: 6 servings

**1-1/2 pounds small fresh beets,
    washed and trimmed
8 tablespoons walnut or olive oil
1/4 cup balsamic vinegar
1 teaspoon brown sugar
3/4 teaspoon toasted and lightly crushed
    anise seeds
Salt and freshly ground pepper
1 small red onion, very thinly sliced
6 tablespoons toasted and coarsely
    chopped walnuts**

**Toppings:
Vegetable oil
12 corn tortillas, cut into 1/4-inch-wide strips

3/4 cup chopped cilantro
1 tablespoon grated lime peel
1 tablespoon fresh lime juice
Small garlic clove, minced

1 cup grated Monterey Jack cheese**

Meanwhile, preheat oven to 350 degrees F. Line a baking sheet with foil and spray with vegetable oil. Arrange tortilla

Heat oven to 400 degrees F. Place beets in a single layer on a large piece of aluminum foil; cover with a second piece of foil and crimp around edges to seal. Roast beets about 1-1/2 hours, or until tender yet somewhat firm when pierced with

CHEF'S CORNER: *Use white and yellow onions for cooked dishes. Sweet Vidalia and red onions are delicious served raw.*

a knife. When cool enough to handle, remove skins by rubbing with a paper towel. Cut off any remaining tops or root ends and cut into thin slices.

In a small bowl, beat together oil, vinegar, brown sugar and anise until well combined. Add salt and pepper to taste. Stir in onion and gently mix in beets. Cover and refrigerate until serving time. The beets are most flavorful after marinating several hours or overnight in the refrigerator.

To serve, place Bibb lettuce leaves on 6 individual salad plates. Divide beet mixture between the plates and sprinkle each salad with toasted chopped walnuts.

Santa Fe Gingerbread with Tangy Poached Apricots

The tang of ginger and the mild heat of chile powder in the gingerbread blends appealingly with the tart, sweet apricots.

Yield: 8 servings

Santa Fe Gingerbread:
1/2 cup butter, softened
1/2 cup dark brown sugar
3/4 cup unsulphered molasses
3 eggs
3 cups all-purpose flour
2 tablespoons ground ginger
1 tablespoon chile powder
1 teaspoon ground nutmeg
1 teaspoon baking soda
3/4 cup buttermilk
1/3 cup orange juice
1 tablespoon grated orange zest
1 teaspoon vanilla extract
1/2 cup heavy cream, whipped and
flavored with vanilla

Preheat oven to 350 degrees F. Grease the bottom of a 9 x 13-inch baking pan. Line with parchment or waxed paper. Grease paper and lightly flour pan.

Place butter and sugar in the bowl of an electric mixer and beat on medium-high speed about 3 minutes, or until mixture is light-colored and fluffy, scraping down two or three times. Stir in molasses and add eggs one at a time, beating well after each addition. Sift dry ingredients together onto a sheet of waxed paper. Combine buttermilk, orange juice, orange zest and vanilla extract in a small bowl. Add flour mixture to butter-and-sugar mixture in three parts, alternating with buttermilk mixture. Beat on low speed after each addition and scrape down sides of bowl with a rubber spatula. Do not overbeat.

Pour batter into prepared pan and bake 30 to 35 minutes, or until a toothpick inserted in the middle comes out clean. Cool 15 minutes, then remove cake from pan and place on a wire rack.

Tangy Poached Apricots:

Yield: about 1 quart
24 fresh whole apricots (can be halved and pitted)

Honey-Flavored Syrup (about 2-1/2 cups):
2 cups honey
1/2 cup water
2 teaspoons freshly grated lemon peel
3 tablespoons lemon juice
1 teaspoon vanilla extract

Combine honey, water, lemon peel and juice in a medium saucepan. Bring to a boil over medium-low heat. Add apricots and simmer 3 to 5 minutes, or until soft (cooking time will depend upon ripeness of fruit). Remove apricots with a slotted spoon and set aside. Add vanilla extract to syrup; when it has cooled, combine with poached apricots. Refrigerate up to one week.

To serve, split individual pieces of gingerbread horizontally and place each bottom piece on a plate. Spread with whipped cream and top with several poached apricots. Replace cake tops and spoon on additional whipped cream, apricots, and syrup.

A Celebration of Pueblo Indian Culture

An Indian Market Supper

Juicy Watermelon Margaritas • Ricotta, Fresh Herb and Poblano Tostadas • Crunchy

Jicama and Citrus Salad • Southwestern Chicken Chili with

Lime Crema • Pumpkin Frybread with Canela Honey • Apricot-Piñon Tart

A Pueblo Corn Dance Feast

Tangy Goat Cheese, Chile and Pumpkin Seed Nachos • Golden Corn and Green Chile

Soup • Minted Zucchini Salad with Lemon-Chile Dressing • Turkey Breast Marinated in Honey, Orange Juice

and Chipotles, with Orange-Cilantro Salsa • Creamy Corn with Scallions and Bacon • Sweet Apple Tamales

A Selection of Dishes Inspired by the Eight Northern Pueblos

Picuris Pueblo—Golden Corn and Green Chile Soup with Vegetable Paints • Taos Pueblo—Braised

Rabbit with Rosemary and Sage • Nambe Pueblo—Piñon-Crusted Trout • San Ildefonso

Pueblo—Refried Black Beans • Tesuque Pueblo—Organic Greens with

Creamy Basil Dressing • San Juan Pueblo—Pueblo Posole • Santa Clara Pueblo—Poached Peaches

with Rose Petal Syrup • Pojoaque Pueblo—Icy Minted Apple Cooler and Apricot Slush

Pueblo is the Spanish word for "village" as well as for the native peoples who inhabit them. New Mexico contains nineteen pueblos, two Apache reservations and a portion of the Diné (Navajo) Reservation. The influence of these Native American groups on daily life in Santa Fe is important culturally and spiritually, as it has been for centuries. Even a commercial venue such as Indian Market seeks to educate the public about Indian peoples and culture and to honor Native arts and artisans.

Indian Market, an event sponsored by the Southwestern Association for Indian Art (SWAIA), is one of August's highlights. It is the largest juried show of American Indian art in the world and draws from across the country more than a thousand traditional and contemporary Native American artists who compete for prizes and sell their work. The weekend event is as interesting to the serious collector of Native American art as it is to the casual visitor because of the wide range of objects displayed and the many fascinating events that are taking place throughout the weekend.

The Plaza is teeming with visitors during Indian Market—some shoppers are actually on the square before dawn to secure a good parking space and preview their favorite artists' work as they set up. No matter what hour you arrive, prepare to be mightily impressed. From the pottery to the silver jewelry, Indian Market features prestigious, top-quality artwork. Clothing style-show competitions, award ceremonies, gala dinners, auctions and the occasional dance exhibition take place all weekend.

While different tribes from all over the country participate in Indian Market, the Pueblo Indians are the indigenous native people of the Santa Fe area. Each pueblo has its own sovereign government, language, and customs and its own traditional feast days and dances throughout the summer. One of the most beautiful of these celebrations is the Corn Dance at the Santo Domingo Pueblo, a community south of Santa Fe. It takes place in August and partly celebrates the corn harvest, the agricultural lifeblood of the Pueblo Indians.

To these people, dances are religious ceremonies; each word and movement is steeped in spiritual significance. To the outsider, it is a magnificent whirl of elaborate traditional clothing, hypnotic song, rhythmic beating of drums, and age-old ritual. The whole pueblo takes part in the Corn Dance in the pueblo's plaza; hundreds of men, women and children perform a ceremony that has remained virtually unchanged for centuries.

After the dances, the feasting takes place in private homes, where traditional foods are shared with friends and family. Pueblo Indian culture and traditional cuisine have inspired the contemporary dishes that follow.

An Indian Market Supper

Indian Market is far more than a commercial event. It is a celebration of the best American Indian arts and crafts in the world. Indian Market features a variety of food vendors, and the fare still focuses on the traditional local crops of grains, corn, beans and chile. Frybread and Indian tacos are always popular at Indian Market. Much of the Indian Market Supper can be prepared ahead of time, so you can enjoy the busy day in town and still eat well when you get home.

Juicy Watermelon Margaritas

This thirst-quenching drink hits the spot and refreshes the spirit after a long day at Indian Market. If a deeper red color is desired, blend 2 to 3 drops of red food coloring with the watermelon.

Yield: 6 servings

4 cups cubed and seeded watermelon
1/2 cup tequila
4 tablespoons superfine sugar
4 tablespoons fresh lime juice
1 tablespoon triple sec
3 cups crushed ice
Lime wedges

Combine first 5 ingredients in a blender and process until smooth. Taste and adjust flavoring. Fill each margarita glass with 1/2 cup crushed ice and top with 1/2 cup puréed watermelon mixture. Garnish glasses with lime wedges.

Ricotta, Fresh Herb and Poblano Tostadas

Tostadas are great finger foods that can have considerably different personalities depending on their toppings. The fresh epazote makes for a delightful flavor boost slightly reminiscent of eucalyptus. The topping is best when served at room temperature.

Yield: 6 servings

3 garlic cloves, roasted and chopped (see p. 26)
2 poblano chiles, roasted, peeled and chopped (see p. 13)
2/3 cup ricotta cheese
1 tablespoon fresh mixed herbs (oregano, thyme, cilantro, epazote), chopped
1 teaspoon fresh lime juice
1/2 teaspoon salt
1/4 teaspoon freshly ground black pepper
6 blue or yellow corn tortillas (see pp. 23–24)
Vegetable oil
1 small avocado, diced
4 large radishes, thinly sliced
1/4 cup sliced scallions with green tops
6 cilantro sprigs

Mix together garlic, chiles, cheese, herbs, lime juice, salt and pepper. Set aside. Heat 1/2 inch of oil in a skillet over medium-high heat. Fry tortillas until crisp but not browned; drain on paper towels. Spoon cheese mixture on each tortilla and top with avocado, radishes, scallions and cilantro.

Note: Serve warm tostadas immediately or they will get soggy.

Crunchy Jicama and Citrus Salad

A tuber indigenous to Mexico and Central America, jicama has a flavor similar to water chestnuts and a delightful crunchy texture. The salad ingredients can be prepared up to 8 hours ahead and then tossed with the dressing just before serving.

Yield: 6 servings

Salad:
1/2 cup thinly sliced red onion
2 pink grapefruits or tangerines
1 small jicama, peeled, sliced and julienned
1/2 small red bell pepper, seeded and julienned
1/2 small yellow bell pepper, seeded and julienned
2 jalapeños, stemmed, seeded and thinly sliced

Rinse onion slices with cold water and drain. Using a sharp knife, peel grapefruit down to the flesh and cut between inner membranes to release grapefruit segments. In a large serving bowl, combine onion, grapefruit, jicama, bell peppers and jalapeños.

Citrus Dressing:
1/4 cup olive or canola oil
3 tablespoons lime juice
1 teaspoon chile caribe (see p. 18)
1 tablespoon honey
2 tablespoons chopped fresh basil leaves
Salt and cayenne pepper to taste

Place oil, lime juice, chile caribe, honey, basil, salt and pepper in a small jar; shake until well mixed. Taste and adjust seasonings, adding more honey to balance acidity of lime juice.

Southwestern Chicken Chili with Lime Crema

Chili probably evolved from simple stews made centuries ago by the Native Americans of the Southwest. The dried chiles can be toasted for an earthy intense flavor or simply rehydrated in a hot liquid for a less-complex flavor. This chili tastes even better when made a day or so before serving. The Lime Crema adds a tangy sparkle to the dish.

Yield: 6 servings

Southwestern Chicken Chili:
4 dried New Mexico red chiles, stemmed and seeded
4 ancho chiles, stemmed and seeded
2 tablespoons vegetable oil
2 cups chopped white onion
6 cloves garlic, chopped
1 pound dried pinto beans, soaked overnight and drained
7 cups chicken broth
2 teaspoons toasted and ground cumin seeds
1 tablespoon chopped fresh oregano leaves
1 teaspoon toasted and ground coriander seeds
2 pounds skinless chicken thighs
Salt to taste
2 tablespoons chopped fresh cilantro (optional)

Cover chiles with boiling water and allow to steep until soft, about 20 minutes. Drain chiles, reserving about 1 cup of liquid. Using a blender, purée chiles with enough reserved liquid to produce a smooth purée.

Heat oil in a skillet over medium heat. Sauté onions until golden; add garlic and sauté until softened. Place beans in a soup pot with chile purée, broth, onions and garlic, cumin, oregano, coriander and chicken. Bring to a boil, reduce heat, and simmer until chicken thighs are cooked, about 30 minutes. Remove chicken and, when cool enough to handle, shred meat and refrigerate.

Continue cooking beans until tender, about 2 hours, adding broth or water if needed. Add shredded chicken to the pot and heat thoroughly. Season with salt and add cilantro. Serve chili in bowls drizzled with Lime Crema.

Lime Crema:
1 cup sour cream
1/4 cup fresh lime juice
2 teaspoons grated lime peel

Whisk together sour cream, lime juice and peel. Season with salt.

Pumpkin Frybread with Canela Honey

Frybread is the traditional bread of the southwestern Indian tribes, and it is always served at markets and on feast days at local pueblos. It is often topped with meat or beans or a sweet spread. The pumpkin adds a rich wholesome flavor as well as a festive orange color. Canela Honey is just right for a sweet and lightly spiced spread.

Yield: about 12 small pieces of frybread

Pumpkin Frybread:
1/2 cup canned pumpkin
1/4 cup honey
1/4 teaspoon salt
1/4 teaspoon cinnamon
1-1/2 cups flour
1 teaspoon baking powder
1/2 cup warm milk
Vegetable oil

Combine pumpkin, honey, salt and cinnamon in a mixing bowl. Combine flour and baking powder; add flour mixture and warm milk to pumpkin mixture, stirring until a soft dough is formed. On a lightly floured surface, knead dough

CHEF'S CORNER: *For light and tender frybread, handle the dough as little as possible, taking care not to overwork it.*

a few times until smooth. (Add a little more flour or milk to adjust texture of dough.) Lightly brush oil over finished dough and allow to rest, covered with a damp cloth, for 20 minutes to 1 hour.

Heat oil in a heavy deep skillet or pot until it reaches 375 degrees F. (Add oil to a depth of 3 inches in a skillet or half the depth of the pot.) With lightly floured hands, pull off golf-ball-sized pieces of dough and pat into rounds 1/2 inch thick, making them a little thinner in the middle. Place on a lightly floured surface. Fry a few at a time, turning often, until golden brown. Drain on absorbent paper towels. Serve piping hot with Canela Honey or powdered sugar.

Canela Honey (1 cup):
1 cup honey
1 teaspoon ground canela
    (or 1/2 teaspoon cinnamon)
1/4 teaspoon allspice
1/4 teaspoon chile powder

Heat honey in a small heavy saucepan over very low heat until warmed. Remove from heat and stir in canela, allspice and chile powder.

Apricot-Piñon Tart

Early Pueblo people harvested piñon nuts from the low-growing piñon pine in the Sangre de Cristo Mountains. Locals today still gather piñon nuts from the ground or shake them from the tree when crops are substantial, about every 4 or 5 years. Peaches can be used instead of apricots, and almonds can replace piñon nuts in this terrific-tasting tart.

Yield: 8 servings
Pastry:
1 cup unbleached white flour
2-1/2 teaspoons sugar
1/4 teaspoon salt
1/2 cup cold unsalted butter, cut into small pieces
1-1/2 to 2 tablespoons ice water

Preheat oven to 450 degrees F. Mix flour, sugar and salt in a food processor fitted with a steel blade. Scatter pieces of butter over flour mixture and process with one-second pulses until mixture resembles oatmeal. Place in a medium bowl and, using a rubber spatula, mix in just enough water to bind dough. Gather pastry into a ball, then flatten into a 1/2-inch-thick disk. Dust lightly with flour, wrap in plastic and chill at least 1 hour.

Allow dough to warm up slightly before pressing into a 9-inch tart pan with removable bottom. Form dough to extend 1/4 inch beyond rim of pan. Fold dough back inside pan and trim off any excess. Pierce pastry shell all over with a fork. Cover with plastic wrap and chill at least 1 hour. (Dough can also be wrapped well and frozen.)

Line shell with waxed paper and weight with raw beans, rice or metal pie weights. Pre-bake until a pale golden brown, about 11 minutes. Remove weights and allow to cool. Reduce oven temperature to 375 degrees F.

Filling:
9 fresh apricots
    (or canned apricot halves, well drained)
1/2 cup apricot jam or preserves
1 tablespoon brandy or rum
1/4 cup toasted piñon nuts (see p. 20)
1 tablespoon butter, cut into small pieces
1/4 cup sugar

To peel apricots, blanch in simmering water about 20 seconds, drain and rinse with cold water. Slip off peels with a paring knife, slice in half, and remove pits.

Mix jam with brandy and spread on bottom of crust. Sprinkle with piñon nuts; arrange apricots cut side down on top of piñon nuts, filling tart shell completely. Dot with butter and sprinkle with sugar. Bake until apricots are tender and filling is syrupy, about 35 minutes. Cool on a wire rack and serve at room temperature.

A Pueblo Corn Dance Feast

Food is the centerpiece of all traditional celebrations. Feasts mark a time of plenty, a communal celebration when friends and family come together to share in nature's bounty and to commemorate collective histories and traditions. It is an honor to be invited to a Pueblo home on feast days. Traditional foods such as posole, horno-baked breads and green chile stews are served, as they have been for generations. The following menu takes its inspiration from the traditional native crops.

Tangy Goat Cheese, Chile, and Pumpkin Seed Nachos

An assertive cheese, spicy chiles and meaty pumpkin seeds top tortillas in this crunchy before-the-meal snack.

Yield: 6 to 8 servings

6 (4-inch) blue or yellow corn tortillas
Vegetable oil
Salt
2 ounces Monterey Jack cheese, grated
4 ounces mild goat cheese, crumbled
4 jalapeños, stemmed, seeded and cut into rings
3 scallions with green tops, sliced
2 tablespoons toasted pumpkin seeds
2 teaspoons red chile powder

Cut tortillas into quarters. Spread in a single layer on a baking pan and cover with a towel to keep from curling; allow to dry until leathery. Heat 1/2-inch oil in a frying pan to 380 degrees F; fry tortillas in small batches until lightly browned and crisp. (See baking alternative on p. 33.) Drain on paper towels and sprinkle lightly with salt.

Preheat broiler to moderate. Arrange tortillas in a single layer on a foil-lined baking sheet. Sprinkle with cheeses, jalapeños, scallions and pumpkin seeds. Dust lightly with red chile powder. Broil until cheeses are melted; serve immediately.

Golden Corn and Green Chile Soup

Corn has been the staff of life in the Southwest for centuries. This is a rich and delicious version of the popular soup found on so many Santa Fe restaurant menus.

Yield: 6 servings

3 cups corn kernels, fresh or frozen
1 cup chicken broth
3 tablespoons unsalted butter
1 cup diced yellow onion
1 clove garlic, minced
1/2 cup diced yellow bell pepper
1 cup diced Roma tomatoes
2 New Mexico green chiles (or Anaheim chiles for milder flavor), roasted, peeled and chopped
1 teaspoon azafran (or 1/2 teaspoon saffron)
1/2 teaspoon toasted and ground coriander
2 cups whole milk (or 1-1/2 cups milk and 1/2 cup heavy cream for richer flavor)
Salt to taste

Place 2 cups of corn in a blender with chicken broth. Reserve remaining cup of corn. Melt butter in a heavy soup pot over medium heat. Sauté onion and yellow pepper 3 minutes, stirring occasionally. Add garlic and sauté until soft. Add tomatoes and continue cooking 5 minutes. Cool slightly. Add cooled mixture to the blender and blend until vegetables are puréed. Strain purée into soup pot, pushing down hard on solids. Stir in reserved corn, chiles, azafran, coriander and milk. Add salt to taste. Simmer gently 15 minutes to prevent curdling.

Variation: Substitute 1 cup cooked chicos for reserved corn. Chicos are whole unhulled kernels of dried corn that add a chewy texture and intense corn flavor to soups and stews. Like dried beans, they must be soaked before cooking (see p. 25).

Minted Zucchini Salad with Lemon-Chile Dressing

Wild mint and squash, two local favorites, combine in this speedy-to-make salad. The ingredients can be prepped ahead and combined just before serving to ensure maximum freshness and color.

Yield: 6 servings

1/4 cup chopped fresh mint leaves
1/4 cup chopped fresh Italian parsley leaves
4 medium-sized zucchini, unpeeled and shredded
6 tablespoons olive or canola oil
3 tablespoons fresh lemon juice
2 teaspoons chili powder
1/4 teaspoon freshly toasted and ground cumin
1 teaspoon honey
Salt and pepper to taste
3 Roma tomatoes, diced

Place mint, parsley and zucchini in a large bowl. Whisk together olive oil, lemon juice, chili powder, cumin and honey in a small bowl. Taste and season with salt and pepper. Toss zucchini mixture with enough dressing to moisten, then scatter tomatoes over the top.

CHEF'S CORNER: *Using a mandoline for shredding vegetables is a real timesaver. Shreds will be uniform in size and will cook quickly and evenly when sautéing.*

Turkey Breast Marinated in Honey, Orange Juice and Chipotles, with Orange-Cilantro Salsa

Wild turkeys were kept and domesticated by the Pueblo peoples. This marinade produces an exceptionally juicy bird whose sweet and slightly smoky flavor is complemented by the bold salsa.

Yield: 6 to 8 servings

Marinade:
2-1/2 cups freshly squeezed orange juice, room temperature
1 cup honey
5 cloves garlic, coarsely chopped
1/4 cup puréed chipotles en adobo with juice (see p. 18)
2 tablespoons vegetable oil

Combine all ingredients in a medium bowl, whisking until well combined.

Turkey Breast:
1 (3- to 4-pound) boneless turkey breast

Place turkey in a large pan and pour on 2-1/2 cups marinade. Reserve remaining marinade for basting. Cover with plastic wrap and refrigerate 4 hours or overnight, turning occasionally to coat turkey with marinade.

Preheat oven to 350 degrees F. Remove turkey from marinade and season with salt and pepper. Place turkey skin side up in a shallow roasting pan. Roast until meat releases clear juices when pricked deeply, or when a meat thermometer registers 160 degree F (approximately 15 to 20 minutes per pound). Baste occasionally with reserved marinade. Remove from oven and let stand 10 minutes. Slice turkey on the diagonal into 1/2-inch-thick slices. Serve with dollops of Orange-Cilantro Salsa.

Orange-Cilantro Salsa:
4 small oranges, peeled, sectioned and chopped
1/4 cup coarsely chopped fresh cilantro
2 serrano chiles, stemmed, seeded and minced
1/2 cup diced red onion
1 teaspoon chopped fresh oregano leaves
3 tablespoons balsamic vinegar
1 tablespoon olive oil
1 teaspoon salt

Combine oranges, cilantro, chiles, onion and oregano in a medium bowl. Drizzle with vinegar and oil; season with salt. Allow to sit at room temperature at least 30 minutes before serving.

Creamy Corn with Scallions and Bacon

This simple sauté is spiced with jalapeño chiles and mellowed with cream and butter.

Yield: 6 servings

2 tablespoons butter or olive oil
3 cups fresh corn kernels (or defrosted frozen corn)
2 jalapeño chiles, stemmed, seeded and thinly sliced
6 scallions, chopped
1/4 cup cooked and crumbled bacon
2 teaspoons minced fresh thyme leaves
1/4 cup heavy cream
Salt and pepper to taste

In a nonstick skillet, heat butter or oil over medium-high heat; sauté and stir corn, jalapeños and scallions 2 minutes. Lower heat and stir in remaining ingredients. Simmer until corn is crisp-tender.

Sweet Apple Tamales

Tamales—cornhusks stuffed with a variety of sweet or savory fillings—can be time-consuming to make until you get the hang of it. Because tamales are often made in large quantities, several people often spend a day working together in their preparation. For a more elaborate dessert, serve these tamales with Coffee Custard Sauce (see p. 140).

Yield: approximately 24 small tamales

Corn Husks:

30 dried cornhusks (more if they are small), including husks used for lining steamer pan

Place cornhusks in a large pot of boiling water. Remove from heat and let stand 30 minutes. Weigh down husks with a plate to keep them submerged. Drain softened husks in a colander and lay them out on towels to dry; keep covered.

Dough:

2 cups masa harina (tamale grind)
1 teaspoon baking powder
1/4 teaspoon salt
1-1/2 teaspoons ground canela
    (or 1 teaspoon ground cinnamon)
1/2 cup packed dark brown sugar
3/4 cup unsalted butter, cut into small pieces
1/2 cup water
1-1/2 cups diced tart apples
1/4 cup golden raisins
1/2 cup chopped pecans

Place masa harina, baking powder, salt, canela and brown sugar in the bowl of an electric mixer or food processor; pulse to blend. Add butter and mix until smooth. Add water and process dough on high speed until light and fluffy (8 to 10 minutes in a mixer or 5 to 6 minutes in a food processor). Place dough in a large bowl and gently stir in apples, raisins and pecans.

To prepare steamer: Place a steamer insert in a large steamer pan; add water to just below bottom of insert. Line insert with a few softened husks.

To form tamales: Tear 2 or 3 husks into long thin strips for tying. On a work surface, lay out a cornhusk with the flat smooth side up. Spread 3 tablespoons of dough in center of husk and flatten slightly into a lengthwise rectangle, leaving at least a 1-1/2-inch border on the tapering end of the husk and a 3/4-inch border along the other sides. Fold sides in. To form a tightly closed "bottom," fold the empty 1-1/2-inch section of tapering end of husk up. Leave top open and loosely tie a strip of husk around the tamale's middle to secure the ends.

As husks are filled, stand the finished tamale in a prepared steamer with folded ends on the bottom. When all husks are filled and placed in the steamer, bring water to a boil, lower heat to a simmer, cover and steam tamales 1 to 1-1/4 hours. Check water level frequently so that pan does not run dry. Tamales are done when the husk peels cleanly away from the dough. Allow tamales to rest 5 minutes before serving.

Note: If cornhusks are small, decrease amount of filling or overlap 2 husks to create the right size. Don't fill husks too full, tie too tightly, or pack tight in steamer as they will expand in steaming. The only way to know if the tamales are ready is to break one open and check for doneness.

CHEF'S CORNER: *Well-wrapped, tamales keep several days refrigerated or a couple of months frozen. To reheat cooked defrosted tamales, use a steamer for best results.*

A Selection of Dishes Inspired by the Eight Northern Pueblos

Of the nineteen pueblos in New Mexico, eight have banded together in a consortium known as the Eight Northern Indian Pueblos Council to maintain and preserve their cultural heritage and share economic opportunities. Each pueblo, a living village, has its own unique history and government, with creative artisans who reflect their customs. The following dishes were developed to honor the Eight Northern Pueblos.

Picuris Pueblo—
Golden Corn and Green Chile Soup with Vegetable Paints

According to archaeologists, Picuris Pueblo has occupied its present location since about A.D. 750. The smallest of all nineteen Pueblo tribes, Picuris has about 350 inhabitants. Its name in the Tewa language means "Those Who Paint."

In this dish, vegetable paints are used to add bright colorful touches to the rims of plates and bowls or to top food. Not merely decorative, they provide a touch of flavor contrast. Using a funnel, pour paints into plastic squeeze bottles. If refrigerated, shake and allow to sit at room temperature 10 minutes before using.

Golden Corn and Green Chile Soup:
(see p. 67 for preparation)

Black Bean Paint:
1 cup cooked black beans
3/4 cup bean broth or water
1 tablespoon chipotles en adobo (see p. 18)
1/2 teaspoon toasted and freshly ground cumin
3/4 teaspoon salt

Purée all ingredients in a blender until very smooth. Push mixture through a fine-mesh strainer into a small bowl. Use a funnel to fill a squeeze bottle with purée.

Red Chile Paint:
1/4 cup finely minced white onion
1 small clove garlic, minced
2 teaspoons vegetable oil
1/4 cup red chile powder
1/4 teaspoon dried Mexican oregano
1-1/4 cups water or broth
Salt to taste

Soften onion and garlic in oil over low heat in a heavy covered pan. Do not brown. Stir in chile powder and oregano. Slowly add water and simmer 15 minutes, or until sauce has thickened to the consistency of heavy cream. Salt to taste. Cool and purée in a blender or food processor. Push purée through a fine-mesh strainer into a small bowl. Use a funnel to fill a squeeze bottle with purée.

To serve: Ladle soup into large rimmed soup bowls. Using "paint"-filled squeeze bottles, apply decorative dots, spirals, squiggles or zigzags to rims of bowls and on top of soup.

Taos Pueblo—
Braised Rabbit with Rosemary and Sage

Located at the base of the Sangre de Cristo Mountains sixty-five miles north of Santa Fe, Taos Pueblo is the most northern Pueblo in New Mexico with the largest surviving multistoried pueblo structure. Taos Pueblo has been the subject of many famous paintings and photographs over the years. Summer rabbit hunts on neighboring mesas have long been a tradition for this community.

Yield: 6 servings
1/4 cup all-purpose flour
1 teaspoon salt
1/2 teaspoon pepper

1 (3- to 3-1/2-pound) rabbit or chicken, cut into serving pieces
3 tablespoons vegetable oil
1 cup peeled pearl onions or chopped yellow onion
2-1/2 cups chicken broth
2 teaspoons minced fresh rosemary leaves
2 teaspoons minced fresh sage leaves
3 juniper berries, lightly bruised
2 tablespoons yellow cornmeal

Combine flour, salt and pepper in a shallow pan; dredge rabbit in mixture. In a heavy Dutch oven, heat 2 tablespoons oil over moderately high heat. Brown rabbit in batches and remove to a plate. Add reserved oil and sauté onions until golden. Reduce heat to low, add rabbit and remaining ingredients except cornmeal, and simmer covered 1 hour. Stir in cornmeal and cook 10 minutes, or until sauce is slightly thickened. Add additional salt and pepper to taste.

CHEF'S CORNER: *To release the aromatic flavor of whole dried spices, bruise them in a mortar with a pestle or on an even surface with the flat side of a heavy knife.*

Piñon Crusted Trout

Nambe Pueblo is home to Nambe Falls, a beautiful and popular recreation area. A herd of buffalo is available for public viewing, and Nambe Lake is stocked with trout, the inspiration for this dish. The nutty, crisp piñon crust perfectly complements the tenderness of the fish.

Yield: 6 servings

1/2 cup piñon nuts, lightly toasted and finely chopped
1/4 cup flour
1 tablespoon sesame seeds
1 teaspoon toasted and ground coriander seeds
1 teaspoon salt
1/2 teaspoon pepper
2 tablespoons vegetable oil, divided
4 tablespoons butter
6 whole boned trout, cleaned, washed, and patted dry with paper towels

Preheat oven to 350 degrees F. Combine piñon nuts, flour, sesame seeds, coriander, salt and pepper. Heat oil and butter in a large heavy frying pan over medium-high heat. Dredge trout on both sides in flour mixture, pressing on coating so it adheres. Sauté 2 minutes on each side, then place on a baking sheet. Sprinkle any remaining flour mixture on top of trout and drizzle with oil from the pan. Bake trout in a preheated oven until opaque in the center.

Note: The secret to a nice crisp crust on trout is the correct cooking temperature. Oil shoud be hot enough to quickly sear the outside coating, keeping the interior moist and flavorful. Don't crowd the pan; if necessary, sauté in batches to maintain oil temperture.

Refried Black Beans

A 26,000-acre pueblo that extends from the Rio Grande to the mountains near Los Alamos, San Ildefonso is famous for its black-on-black pottery. Beans—as well as corn, squash, wheat and other crops—grow in fields outside the village and constitute a main food source for the pueblo.

Yield: 6 servings

1/4 cup lard or peanut oil
1/2 cup minced white onion
5 cloves garlic, minced
1-1/2 teaspoons salt
3 cups cooked or canned black beans, rinsed and drained (for cooking dried beans, see p. 25)
2 tablespoons minced fresh epazote
1-1/2 teaspoons toasted and ground cumin
1 teaspoon toasted and ground coriander seed
1/4 cup grated queso fresco or asadero cheese

Heat lard or oil in large skillet over medium heat. Sauté onions until golden; add garlic and cook until tender. Mash beans with a potato masher or the back of a heavy wooden spoon until smooth. Stir remaining ingredients except cheese into beans. Increase heat to medium-high and add bean mixture to skillet. Continue cooking, stirring frequently, until beans pull away from sides of pan. Sprinkle with cheese and serve immediately.

Organic Greens with Creamy Basil Dressing

The closest Pueblo to Santa Fe, Tesuque Pueblo owns the Tesuque Pueblo Flea Market, a weekend shopping institution amongst locals. Organic produce is grown on their sixty-acre farm and sold in town at the Farmers' Market. Exotic lettuces and herbs are the specialties grown there.

Yield: 6 servings

Organic Greens:

**3 small heads assorted organic lettuces, washed
and dried very well**

**3 cups assorted chopped or shredded vegetable
toppings (carrots, baby beets, cherry tomatoes,
crisp-cooked green beans, celery, radishes,
green onions)**

**1/4 cup assorted chopped fresh herbs (parsley,
cilantro, chives, thyme, oregano, or dill)**

Tear lettuce into bite-sized pieces and place in large salad
bowl. Place vegetables on top of lettuce and sprinkle with
herbs. Spread a thick layer of Creamy Basil Dressing over
top of salad. Cover bowl tightly with plastic wrap and chill
in refrigerator several hours. Toss gently before serving,
adding more dressing if necessary.

Creamy Basil Dressing:

2 tablespoons firmly packed fresh basil leaves

1/2 cup mayonnaise

1/4 cup plain yogurt or sour cream

3 green onions with green tops, sliced

1 clove garlic, coarsely chopped

1-1/2 teaspoons cider vinegar

1 teaspoon sugar

1/4 teaspoon dry mustard

Salt and freshly ground black pepper to taste

Combine all ingredients in a food processor and process until
smooth. There will be some extra dressing for another use.

San Juan Pueblo—
Pueblo Posole

The largest pueblo in northern New Mexico, San Juan Pueblo is situated on the fertile ground where the Rio Grande and the Chama River come together. The pueblo has an agricultural cooperative that serves the residents and helps coordinate commercial ventures.

Posole—dried corn that has been boiled with a solution of slaked lime and water—refers to the uncooked corn as well as the dish. Traditionally, posole is made with pork but is often served without meat as a side dish.

Yield: 6 cups

2 tablespoons vegetable oil
1 cup chopped white onion
2 cloves garlic, chopped
1 cup dried or 1-1/2 cups frozen posole, rinsed well before cooking
3 dried New Mexico red chile pods
2 teaspoons dried Mexican oregano
2 teaspoons salt
8 cups unsalted chicken broth or water
Chopped cilantro

If using dried posole, soak 4 hours or overnight.

Heat oil in a large pot over medium heat. Sauté onion until pale golden; add garlic and sauté 1 minute. Place remaining ingredients in pot and bring to a boil. Reduce heat and cook over low heat approximately 2 hours, or until posole is puffed and tender with most of the liquid absorbed. Add additional liquid during cooking time if necessary. Remove and discard chiles, or chop and add to posole.

Variation: Add 1 pound of cubed pork stew meat during second hour of cooking.

Santa Clara Pueblo—
Poached Peaches with Rose Petal Syrup

Santa Clara Pueblo encompasses 46,000 acres of beautiful mesas, canyons, caves and lush valleys. Nearby is Puye Cliffs whose cliff dwellings were the ancestral home of the Santa Clara Pueblo people. This pueblo is known in Tewa as "Valley of the Wild Roses." Use unsprayed roses from the garden for this dish. Nectarines or apricots can be substituted for peaches.

Yield: 6 servings

Rose Petal Syrup:
2-1/4 cups water
3/4 cup sugar
1 canela or cinnamon stick
8 roses, petals removed and washed

Stir water and sugar together in a heavy medium saucepan over medium heat until sugar dissolves. Add canela and rose petals; reduce heat and simmer 10 minutes. Remove from heat and allow mixture to steep at room temperature 1 hour; strain through a coarse sieve.

Poached Peaches:
6 peaches, peeled
1 teaspoon pure vanilla extract
    (or 1/2 teaspoon almond extract)

Cut peaches in half; place halves, pits and syrup together in a saucepan. Simmer until peaches are barely tender. Remove from heat, stir in vanilla and refrigerate until serving time.

To serve, place Poached Peaches with a little of the Rose Petal Syrup in glass serving bowls; generously garnish with fresh rose petals.

Note: Some varieties of roses have a bitter white flesh at the base of the petals; taste before using and cut away if necessary. For a more intense rose flavor, add 1 teaspoon rosewater with vanilla extract.

Pojoaque Pueblo—
Icy Minted Apple Cooler and Apricot Slush

In the Tewa language, Pojoaque Pueblo is known as **Po-suwae-geh,** *meaning "Water-Drinking Place." The pueblo's history of hospitality is recognized here with two cold drinks made from local apples, apricots and water— the area's most precious natural resource.*

Icy Minted Apple Cooler (6 servings):
6 cups unfiltered apple cider
1-1/2 cups fresh mint leaves, washed
7 tablespoons sugar
1 cup peeled and finely diced tart apple
2 tablespoons fresh lime juice
2 cups ice cubes
Mint sprigs

Bring apple cider to a boil in a medium saucepan; cook until reduced by half. Place mint and sugar in large bowl and crush with the back of a spoon. Pour cider over mint and steep until cooled. Strain mixture through a fine sieve into a blender, pressing down on mint leaves with a rubber spatula. Add remaining ingredients and blend until smooth. Garnish with mint.

Apricot Slush (6 or more servings):
24 large fresh ripe apricots, cut in half and pitted
2 teaspoons fresh lemon juice
1/2 cup sugar (or to taste)
48 ounces cold soda water

Purée apricots, lemon juice and sugar in a blender until very smooth. Strain into a bowl, then pour into ice cube trays and freeze. Using a blender, purée apricot cubes in small batches with enough soda water to make a slushy consistency. Pour into a large pitcher and stir in remaining soda water. Serve in tall chilled glasses.

Note: This healthy summer drink is bursting with vitamins. In the warm days of July, the peak of apricot season in northern New Mexico, it is a vibrant and welcome refresher.

Rodeos, Cookouts and Barbecues

A Rodeo Barbecue

Tequila-Spiked Caesar Salad with Achiote-Flavored Tortilla Frizzles • Grilled Chile-Marinated Rib-Eye

Steaks • A Sizzling Bowl of Black Beans • Grilled Peppered Zucchini, Yellow Onions and Fennel • Assorted

Fresh Berries with Vanilla Velvet Cream • Chocolate 'n' Cream Brownies

A Fourth of July Cookout

Red-and-Green Coleslaws with Jicama and Dill • Cascabel-Marinated Baby Back Ribs • Santa Fe

Crispy Cornmeal Fried Chicken • Grilled Sweet Potato Salad with Basil Vinaigrette • Red, White and

Blueberry Pound Cakes • Frozen Chocolate-Banana Popsicles

A Southwestern Lamb Barbecue

Arugula and Papaya Salad with Toasted Pepitas and Lime Vinaigrette • Grilled Butterflied

Leg of Lamb with Apple-Chipotle Chutney • "The City Different" Ratatouille • Piñon-Crusted

Bread Strips • Banana and Strawberry Chocolate-Crêpe Burritos

Cow [...] going to St.[...]

The rodeo is as quintessentially American as the cowboy, apple pie, cookouts and barbecues. For more than fifty years, the Rodeo de Santa Fe has been one of the city's major summer events. But the sports of bronc and bull riding, calf roping and steer wrestling started long before that. In the old days, ranch hands and Spanish vaqueros used to compete in these activities just for fun and recognition among their peers. Today, professional associations govern the three-day program that draws hundreds of international visitors.

The rodeo grounds are jammed with enthusiasts before the show, and the scent of barbecue hangs in the cloudless blue sky. Rodeo fans weave their fingers through the fence links of the stock pens and study the animals, old-timers reminisce about their cowboy days, teenagers show off for one another on the mechanical bull, and kids in ten-gallon hats twice their size kick up dust clouds with their cowboy boots. Programs are hawked, food vendors shout enticements at passersby, and tee shirts commemorating the rodeo are offered, adding to the carnival atmosphere. Country music blasts over the loudspeakers as the crowd settles into seats and the show begins.

As the sun drops over the Sangre de Cristo Mountains, Miss Rodeo de Santa Fe and her court—all dressed in flamboyant costumes—circle the ring, riding their horses at breakneck speeds. The country's fastest steer wrestlers and calf ropers compete for honors and payback money. Young children compete in "mutton bustin' "—riding big sheep intent on shaking them off. Last is the main event, the bull riders. The bulls rush out of the bucking chutes, twisting and spinning madly; the cowboys, hanging onto a rope tied around the bull's girth, must endure these bone-breaking gyrations for eight seconds just to receive a score. The performances of these world-class athletes are remarkable. The rodeo is not just a show but a way of life for them.

Another popular family event is the Fourth of July Pancake Breakfast on the Plaza and its corresponding entertainment that has been a tradition since the Bicentennial. The event is a sprawling community picnic whose proceeds benefit selected charities. The syrup-scented Plaza is invaded with dozens of volunteers flipping flapjacks in tents to serve the hundreds of hungry patrons lining the streets.

Elsewhere in the nation, Independence Day is celebrated with parades marching down main streets and fireworks lighting up the night sky. In Santa Fe, the celebrations are more low-key, reflecting the area's historical experience. In 1776, when East Coast colonials had declared their independence from England, the New Mexico area was still a territory of Spain. Accordingly, Independence Day held little significance for the locals and is a relatively quiet event in Santa Fe today.

Family parties—particularly cookouts and barbecues—are the biggest social events on locals' Fourth of July calendars. Grills are fired up, and platters are heaped with down-home cooking, southwestern style.

A Rodeo Barbecue

Barbecue is traditionally associated with the rodeo. There's something about the heartiness of a barbecue that complements the vigorous sportsmanship of the rodeo's performers. Those western favorites—steak and beans—are at the centerpiece of this classic American menu.

Tequila-Spiked Caesar Salad with Achiote-Flavored Tortilla Frizzles

In this unique Caesar salad, romaine is jazzed up with a tangy dressing, which is topped off with colorful, crunchy tortilla strips.

Yield: 6 servings

Caesar Salad:
1 head romaine lettuce (inner leaves only), cleaned and torn into bite-sized pieces
2 small avocados, diced
1 small red onion, diced
3 Roma tomatoes, cut into quarters
1/2 cup shaved Parmesan cheese

Combine all salad ingredients except cheese in a large bowl. Add just enough dressing to the salad to lightly moisten. Top individual servings with cheese and Achiote-Flavored Tortilla Frizzles.

Caesar Dressing:
1/4 cup reduced-fat sour cream
1/2 cup canola oil
1/4 cup fresh lime juice
2 tablespoons tequila
1/4 cup chopped fresh cilantro or parsley
1 teaspoon chile caribe (see p. 18)
1 tablespoon chile powder
2 teaspoons minced garlic
Salt and freshly ground black pepper to taste

Whisk dressing ingredients together until smooth.

Tortilla Frizzles:
1 clove garlic, halved
2 teaspoons achiote paste* (see p. 17)
3 corn tortillas
2 tablespoons canola oil
Salt to taste

Preheat oven to 400 degrees F. In a small skillet, heat oil over medium-low heat; add garlic clove and achiote paste. Stir and sauté 1 minute, remove from heat and cool. Strain oil through a fine sieve or cheesecloth. Using a pastry brush, lightly coat both sides of tortillas with flavored oil. Stack tortillas and cut into thin strips. Place strips in a single layer on a nonstick baking sheet. Salt lightly and bake until crisp.

Achiote, the seed of the annatto tree native to South America, is often used to season chicken, pork, fish or rice. It is also used as a yellow-to-red coloring agent for food products and fabrics.

Grilled Chile-Marinated Rib-Eye Steaks

The scent and sizzle of these chile-enhanced steaks barbecuing on the grill will make your mouth water! Lime juice in the marinade adds zest to the hearty flavor of the meat.

Yield: 6 steaks
6 (8-ounce) rib-eye steaks

Chile Marinade:
3 tablespoons olive oil
2 cloves garlic, minced
2 tablespoons chile powder
1 tablespoon paprika
1 teaspoon toasted and ground cumin seeds
1/2 teaspoon dried oregano
1/2 teaspoon coarsely ground black pepper
1/4 cup fresh lime juice

Warm olive oil in a small skillet over medium heat. Add garlic, chile powder, cumin and dried oregano. Cook 1 minute, stirring constantly. Allow to cool, then add remaining ingredients. Pour marinade over steaks in a shallow baking dish, turning steaks to coat both sides. Cover and refrigerate 4 hours. Remove steaks from marinade and pat dry with a paper towel. Grill to desired doneness.

A Sizzling Bowl of Black Beans

Black beans, also known as turtle beans, stand up well to the smoky flavors of the chipotles.

Yield: 10 servings
1 pound black beans, cleaned and rinsed
4 tablespoons lard, olive oil or peanut oil
1 large white onion, chopped
2 cloves garlic, chopped
3 chipotle chiles
1 teaspoon toasted and ground cumin seed
1 teaspoon dried epazote
1 large bay leaf
1 teaspoon salt*
Sherry vinegar to taste
3 scallions, chopped
1/2 cup crumbled ricotta salata or mild feta cheese

Soak beans overnight in 3 quarts water. Drain beans; place in heavy pot with enough water to cover by 2 inches. Heat oil in a skillet over medium-high heat. Add onion and sauté until golden. Add garlic and sauté 1 minute. Add onion and garlic, chiles, cumin, epazote and bay leaf to beans; cover and simmer until beans are done, about 2 hours. To avoid burning beans, stir occasionally and add water as necessary.

Add salt and sherry vinegar the last 10 minutes of cooking. Remove bay leaf and chipotle chiles before serving. (If desired, chop and return chiles to the pot of beans.) Serve beans hot, garnished with scallions and crumbled cheese.

Add salt to beans after they are fully cooked or the skins will be tough. The amount of cooking time depends upon the freshness of the dried beans and the elevation at which they are cooked.

Grilled Peppered Zucchini, Yellow Onions and Fennel

The herbaceous flavor of the marinade infuses the vegetables with a terrific taste. Serve hot or as a cool side dish drizzled with some of the marinade.

Yield: 6 servings

Marinade:

1/2 cup olive oil

1/4 cup chopped, tightly packed, mixed fresh herbs (basil, thyme, or cilantro leaves)

2 teaspoons salt

1 teaspoon coarsely ground black pepper

1/4 cup fresh lemon juice

Vegetables:

3 medium zucchini, trimmed and sliced lengthwise into 1/4-inch-thick slices

1 large yellow onion, trimmed and sliced crosswise into 1/4-inch-thick slices

1 large fennel bulb, peeled and sliced lengthwise into 1/4-inch-thick slices

In a large bowl, whisk all marinade ingredients together. Toss vegetables in marinade and let sit at room temperature 30 minutes to 1 hour. Grill over medium-hot fire about 2 minutes on each side, or until slightly charred and soft to the touch.

Assorted Fresh Berries with Vanilla Velvet Cream

This delectable dessert showcases sweet seasonal berries, and a foamy cream topping adds a cool finish.

Yield: 6 servings

Berries:

3 baskets assorted berries, cleaned and dried

Sugar, if needed

Slice berries; combine in a large bowl, adding a little sugar if berries are too tart.

Vanilla Velvet Cream:

1 cup confectioners' sugar

3 tablespoons melted butter

1 egg yolk*

    (or 1/4 cup pasteurized egg substitute)

    *(see p. 53 if using uncooked eggs in a recipe)

1 teaspoon vanilla extract

Pinch of salt

1 cup heavy cream

Ground canela or cinnamon

CHEF'S CORNER: *To simplify any grilling process, roast prepared vegetables in a grill basket alongside a choice of meats.*

In a medium bowl, beat together sugar, butter, egg yolk, vanilla and salt. In a separate bowl, whip cream until soft peaks form, then fold into sugar mixture. Top individual servings of berries with Vanilla Velvet Cream and dust lightly with canela.

Chocolate 'n' Cream Brownies

Comfort food for the kid in all of us, these brownies are a delicious indulgence. These treats make it easy for guests to serve themselves.

Yield: 18 small brownies
Preheat oven to 350 degrees F.

Chocolate Mixture:
3 tablespoons unsalted butter
4 ounces bittersweet baking chocolate

In a small heavy saucepan, melt the chocolate and butter over low heat; stir to combine. Remove from heat and set aside.

Cream Cheese Mixture:
2 tablespoons softened
    unsalted butter
3 ounces cream cheese,
    room temperature
1/4 cup sugar
1 egg
1 tablespoon flour
1 teaspoon canela (or 1/2
    teaspoon cinnamon)
1 teaspoon vanilla extract

In the medium bowl of an electric mixer, cream butter and cream cheese until fluffy. Beat sugar, egg, flour, canela and vanilla into creamed mixture; set aside.

Chocolate Batter:
2 eggs
3/4 cup sugar
1/2 cup flour
1/2 teaspoon baking powder
1/2 teaspoon salt
1/2 cup chopped pecans or walnuts
2 ounces coarsely chopped semisweet chocolate
1 teaspoon vanilla extract
1/2 teaspoon almond extract

Beat eggs with sugar until blended. Mix flour, baking powder and salt together, then stir into egg-and-sugar mixture; add cooled chocolate mixture, nuts, chocolate and extracts.

Grease a 9-inch square baking pan. Spread half the chocolate batter evenly over the bottom. Spread cream-cheese mixture over chocolate batter; drop spoonfuls of remaining chocolate batter over the top. Cut through top of batter with a knife to give a marbled effect. Bake 50 minutes, or until a toothpick inserted in the center comes out clean. Cool before cutting.

A Fourth of July Cookout

After celebrating Independence Day with music and dancing on the Plaza, a cookout is next on the agenda for most Santa Feans. Enjoying a meal al fresco with family and friends is the perfect way to wind up a Fourth of July celebration. So light up some sparklers and fire up the grill for barbecued ribs and southwestern fried chicken!

Red-and-Green Coleslaws with Jicama and Dill

This is a refreshing and colorful approach to an old favorite. For a unique twist, sprinkle with toasted whole cumin seeds before serving.

Yield: 6 to 8 servings

Red Coleslaw:
1/2 head red cabbage, shredded
2 tablespoons finely chopped fresh dill
1/4 cup finely chopped red onion
1/2 cup chopped celery

Green Coleslaw:
1/2 head green cabbage, shredded
2 carrots, peeled and shredded
1/2 medium jicama, peeled and shredded
1/4 cup chopped scallions
1/2 cup chopped cilantro

In one bowl, combine red cabbage, dill, red onion and celery. In another bowl, toss green cabbage with remaining salad ingredients.

Coleslaw Dressing:
1 cup orange or pineapple juice
1/4 cup fresh lime juice
3/4 cup vegetable oil
2 teaspoons hot pepper sauce (optional)
Salt and freshly cracked black pepper to taste

Whisk dressing ingredients together in a small bowl until well combined.

Toss each bowl of vegetables with enough dressing to moisten. Mound green coleslaw in the center of a large platter and surround it with red coleslaw.

Cascabel-Marinated Baby Back Ribs

What's a cookout without ribs? This piquant sauce gets its kick from the earthy, nutty-flavored cascabel chiles. For a flavor boost, bake the ribs the day before and marinate them in the sauce overnight before the final grilling.

Yield: 6 to 8 servings

Ribs:
6 pounds baby back ribs
Garlic salt and pepper

Preheat oven to 350 degrees F. Season both sides of ribs with garlic salt and pepper. Place in a roasting pan, add 3 cups of water, cover with aluminum foil, and bake until tender, about 1 hour.

Cascabel Sauce:
1 cup brown sugar
1/2 cup chili sauce
1/2 cup cascabel (see p. 14) purée
1/4 cup soy sauce
1/2 cup dark beer
1/4 cup cider vinegar
1/2 teaspoon freshly toasted and ground cumin
1 teaspoon ground allspice
Salt to taste

Mix remaining ingredients together in a small saucepan and simmer over very low heat 5 minutes.

Drain ribs, place on a large sheet pan in a single layer and baste with sauce. Prepare a barbecue for grilling over medium heat. Grill ribs about 20 minutes, or until they reach the desired doneness, basting with sauce and turning frequently.

Note: If ribs have been marinated in the refrigerator overnight, bring them to room temperature before final grilling.

Santa Fe Crispy Cornmeal Fried Chicken

For those who like a little kick to their food, this chile-spiced chicken is just the thing. Finishing the chicken in the oven makes the coating extra crunchy.

Yield: 4 to 6 servings

Chicken:
1 fryer chicken, cut into parts and rinsed in water
2 cups buttermilk
2 tablespoons minced chipotles en adobo with sauce (see p. 18)

Stir buttermilk and chipotles together. Pour into a large plastic bag and add chicken pieces. Marinate 4 hours or overnight in refrigerator.

Coating:
2 teaspoons salt
2 teaspoons garlic powder
1 teaspoon freshly toasted and ground cumin
2 teaspoons red chile powder
1-1/2 cups all-purpose flour
1/4 cup yellow cornmeal

Mix salt, garlic powder, cumin, chile powder, flour and cornmeal together in a sealable plastic bag.

Remove chicken from marinade and drain briefly. Place 3 or 4 pieces of chicken in bag and shake to coat well. Transfer chicken to a platter and repeat with remaining pieces. Refrigerate 30 minutes.

Preheat oven to 350 degrees F. Pour canola oil into a large heavy skillet to a depth of 1 inch; heat to 350 degrees F. Add chicken pieces and fry, turning frequently until chicken is evenly golden brown, about 6 minutes. Transfer browned chicken to a rack set over a rimmed baking sheet. Bake chicken about 30 minutes, or until fully cooked. Drain chicken on paper towels to absorb any excess oil.

Grilled Sweet Potato Salad with Basil Vinaigrette

Both savory and sweet, this colorful salad mingles simple flavors in a delightful way. Dress the potatoes while still warm so they will absorb the flavors of the vinaigrette.

Yield: 6 servings

Sweet Potato Salad:

4 sweet potatoes, peeled and cut into 1/2-inch slices

1/4 cup olive oil

1/2 cup red bell pepper, seeded and diced

1/2 cup sliced green onions with bulb and green tops

1/4 cup roughly chopped flat-leaf parsley

1/4 cup cooked and crumbled crisp bacon

Preheat grill to medium. Brush both sides of sweet potato slices with olive oil. Grill potatoes until tender, about 4 minutes on each side. Cool slightly and cut into 1-inch cubes. Combine potatoes with diced pepper, onion, parsley and bacon.

Basil Vinaigrette:

3/4 cup olive oil

2 tablespoons red wine vinegar

2 tablespoons balsamic vinegar

2 tablespoons fresh lemon juice

1 tablespoon Worcestershire sauce

1 tablespoon Dijon mustard

1 teaspoon sugar

1 teaspoon minced garlic

1/4 cup roughly chopped fresh basil

Salt and freshly cracked pepper to taste

In a small bowl, combine garlic and mustard; add olive oil in a slow stream, whisking constantly. Add remaining ingredients and mix well. Pour vinaigrette over sweet potato mixture and toss gently.

Red, White and Blueberry Pound Cakes

Raspberries are red, blueberries are blue, and a garnish of confectioners' sugar is the white in these patriotic pound cakes.

Yield: 2 cakes

3 cups sugar

1-1/2 cups butter, room temperature

10 large eggs, separated

1 teaspoon vanilla extract

1 teaspoon cream of tartar

3 cups all-purpose flour

1 cup blueberries, cleaned and patted dry

1 cup raspberries, cleaned and patted dry

Confectioners' sugar

Preheat oven to 325 degrees F. Grease two 9-1/2 x 5-1/2-inch loaf pans and line with waxed paper. Using an electric mixer, cream sugar and butter until light and fluffy, about 15 minutes. Add egg yolks and vanilla and beat until well blended. In a large mixing bowl, beat egg whites until foamy. Add cream of tartar and continue to beat until whites form soft peaks. Blend whites and flour alternately into butter mixture, a fourth of each at a time. Mix well after each addition.

Place half the cake batter in another large bowl. Gently stir blueberries into one bowl of cake batter and the raspberries into the other. Pour batter into loaf pans. Bake about 1-1/2 hours, or until a wooden pick inserted in middle of cake comes out clean. Place on a wire rack to cool 5 minutes. Invert cakes and remove waxed paper. Place cakes on rack to cool completely. Sift confectioners' sugar over cakes just before serving.

Note: To prevent berries from sinking to the bottom of a cake or a muffin, add half the berries to batter mixture and distribute remaining half over the top before baking. They will sink in during baking.

Frozen Chocolate-
Banana Popsicles

Kids love these and so do adults!

Yield: 6 bananas

8 ounces bittersweet or semisweet chocolate,
cut into chunks
1/2 cup chopped roasted peanuts
1/2 cup shredded coconut
6 small ripe bananas, peeled
6 Popsicle sticks

Place chocolate in a glass pie pan and microwave uncovered on medium power about 2 minutes; stir. Continue to microwave and stir at 1-minute intervals until 2/3 of the chocolate is melted. Remove from microwave and stir until remaining chocolate is melted. (The chocolate can also be melted in a small pan over very low heat.)

Place peanuts and coconut on separate squares of waxed paper. Insert Popsicle sticks lengthwise in bananas. Roll bananas, one at a time, in chocolate, then in peanuts and coconut. Place on a wire rack and allow to set for a few minutes. Wrap each banana in plastic wrap and place in a plastic bag in the freezer.

A Southwestern Lamb Barbecue

Since Spanish explorers introduced sheep into the region in the 1500s, lamb has been a special feature of Santa Fe cuisine. An interesting salad, flavorful vegetables, hearty bread and a simple dessert are perfect partners with the lamb.

Toss arugula with Lime Vinaigrette and divide among 6 salad plates. Arrange fruit slices on arugula; top with cheese and pepitas.

Lime Vinaigrette:
2 tablespoons fresh lime juice
1 teaspoon freshly grated lime peel
3 tablespoons rice vinegar
6 tablespoons grapeseed or extra virgin olive oil
Salt and freshly ground black pepper to taste

Mix lime juice and peel with rice vinegar in a small bowl. Whisk in oil until well combined. Add salt and pepper to taste.

Arugula and Papaya Salad with Toasted Pepitas and Lime Vinaigrette

What better proof of just how great a salad can be! The combination of salty, sweet, and peppery flavors is a remarkable trio.

Yield: 6 servings
Arugula and Papaya Salad:
6 cups arugula leaves or watercress, cleaned and torn into bite-sized pieces
2 small papayas, pears or mangos, peeled and cut into slices
1/2 cup crumbled Gorgonzola cheese
1/4 cup toasted and salted pepitas (see p. 20)

Grilled Butterflied Leg of Lamb with Apple-Chipotle Chutney

Enhanced by chiles, citrus and local wine, the marinade imparts vigorous flavors to the tender succulent lamb. Chipotles provide underlying notes of fiery, smoky flavor to the bold sweet-hot chutney, which will also wake up grilled pork tenderloin and sautéed chicken cutlets.

Yield: 6 to 8 servings
Marinade:
1 cup dry red wine
1/2 cup fresh orange juice
1/4 cup lemon juice

1/2 cup olive oil

2 tablespoons honey

2 tablespoons ancho chile powder

2 tablespoons minced chipotles en adobo (see p. 18)

1/2 cup coarsely chopped white onion

4 cloves garlic, coarsely chopped

1 (7-pound) leg of lamb, butterflied
  (net weight: 5 pounds)

Combine all ingredients in a food processor fitted with a steel blade or in a blender; process 20 seconds. Place lamb in a large nonreactive roasting pan and pour on marinade. Refrigerate 12 to 24 hours, turning meat occasionally.

Preheat grill to high (fire should be very hot). Remove lamb from marinade and place on grill 3 inches from flame. Grill on each side for about 20 minutes for medium-rare to medium. (For best flavor and texture, meat should be pink in the middle.) Remove to a wooden cutting board and allow to stand a few minutes before slicing against the grain in diagonal slices. Serve with Apple-Chipotle Chutney.

Apple-Chipotle Chutney (about 4 cups):

1 tablespoon olive oil

1/4 cup chopped red onion

1 clove garlic, minced

1 tablespoon grated fresh ginger

1 cup fresh orange juice

6 tablespoons red wine vinegar

1/2 cup packed light brown sugar

2 tablespoons honey

4 Granny Smith apples, peeled, cored and diced

1 red bell pepper, chopped

5 chipotle peppers, stemmed and seeded

2 poblano chiles, roasted, peeled and chopped

Heat olive oil in a nonreactive saucepan over medium heat. Sauté onion and garlic until soft. Add remaining ingredients and simmer uncovered over low heat until thick, about 30 minutes. Stir often to prevent scorching, adding a little orange juice if necessary. Remove softened chipotles, chop and stir into chutney.

"The City Different" Ratatouille

Zucchini and eggplant star in this healthy dish that features a profusion of garden-ripe vegetables. The quantities of the vegetables are not absolutes, so work with whatever combinations you like best.

Yield: 6 servings

1/4 cup olive oil

1-1/2 cups coarsely chopped white onions

1 tablespoon finely minced garlic

3 medium zucchini, cut into 3/4-inch cubes

1-1/2 pounds small eggplants, unpeeled and cut
  into 3/4-inch cubes

1-1/4 pounds Roma tomatoes, cut into 1-inch cubes

3 poblano chiles, roasted, peeled and cut into
  1-inch squares

1 teaspoon finely chopped fresh thyme
  (or 1/2 teaspoon dried thyme)

1 teaspoon finely chopped fresh oregano
  (or 1/2 teaspoon dried oregano)

1 teaspoon finely chopped fresh rosemary leaves
  (or 1/2 teaspoon dried rosemary)

1 bay leaf

Salt and freshly ground pepper to taste

2 tablespoons chopped parsley

Heat oil in a heavy saucepan over medium heat. Add onions; sauté and stir until golden. Add garlic and sauté 1 minute. Remove onions and garlic and set aside. Add zucchini and eggplant to pan; sauté 5 minutes, shaking pan and stirring. Add reserved onions and garlic, tomatoes, chiles, thyme, oregano, rosemary and bay leaf. Season with salt and pepper; stir to blend. Cook over low heat 10 minutes. Remove bay leaf and sprinkle with parsley before serving.

Piñon-Crusted Bread Strips

This bread has a distinctive rich flavor and a beautiful red-dish glow from a glaze made with red chile powder. It is cut into strips for serving ease.

Yield: 12 to 14 slices

2 (1/4-ounce) envelopes active dry yeast
1/2 teaspoon sugar
1/2 cup lukewarm water
1/2 cup dry white wine
1/4 cup fruity olive oil
1-1/2 cups whole wheat flour
1-1/4 cups unbleached all-purpose flour
1/4 cup rye flour
2 teaspoons salt
1 teaspoon red chile powder
2 tablespoons water
1/2 cup piñon nuts

Stir yeast and sugar into warm water and let stand 10 minutes. Add wine and oil. Mix flours with salt; place all except 1 cup in large bowl of an electric mixer. Slowly pour in yeast mixture and, using the dough hook, mix on low. Gradually stir in remaining flour and knead in mixer on low speed until dough is smooth and elastic, about 8 minutes. Turn dough out on a floured board and knead by hand 2 minutes. (If dough seems dry, knead in a little water; if it is very sticky, knead in a few tablespoons of flour.) Place dough in a large oiled bowl; turn over to coat entire surface with oil. Cover with a damp cloth and let rise in a warm place, at least 3 hours or overnight.

CHEF'S CORNER: *If not using an electric mixer on yeast breads, combine flour and liquid mixtures with a heavy spoon and knead by hand until dough is smooth and silky, about eight minutes.*

Punch down dough and knead 1 minute on a lightly floured surface. Shape with hands into a rectangle, about 12 inches long and 1/2 inch thick. Let rise again in a warm place until nearly doubled in volume, about 1-1/2 hours.

While dough is rising, mix chile powder with water and, using a pastry brush, paint it over the surface of the dough. Sprinkle piñon nuts over surface and press in gently with fingers. Slide dough onto a greased baking sheet (or heated baking stone) and bake in a preheated 375-degree F oven until bread is lightly browned and firm to the touch, about 35 minutes. Set bread on a rack to cool. Using a serrated knife, slice into 1-inch-wide strips, brush generously with olive oil, and serve warm.

Banana and Strawberry Chocolate-Crêpe Burritos

Serve one crêpe burrito of each flavor for a winning dessert combination.

Yield: 16 crêpe burritos

Chocolate-Crêpe Batter:
1 cup all-purpose flour
3 tablespoons unsweetened cocoa powder
3 tablespoons sugar
1 teaspoon ground canela
　　(or 1/2 teaspoon cinnamon)
1/4 teaspoon salt
1/2 cup water
1/2 cup milk
3 large eggs
2 tablespoons unsalted butter, melted and cooled
Clarified butter or canola oil

In a blender or food processor, blend all ingredients about 15 seconds. (Batter can be made a day ahead and refrigerated until 1 hour before cooking.) Stir batter and add more milk if it needs thinning.

Brush a nonstick 6- to 7-inch-diameter skillet liberally with butter and heat until hot. Select a large spoon that will hold about 2 tablespoons of batter; pour a spoonful of batter in the pan, and roll it around quickly until the bottom is completely covered (tip out any excess batter). As soon as batter appears dull and the edges have begun to brown, use a spatula to flip the crêpe onto the other side. The second side will cook more quickly. Remove first crêpe from pan and throw it away (it absorbs the butter and doesn't taste very good). Make rest of crêpes with remaining batter in the same manner, adding more butter to pan only if crêpes begin to stick.

Note: Crêpes can be made 3 days in advance; keep stacked and well-wrapped in plastic wrap in the refrigerator. They also freeze well.

Banana Filling:
2 tablespoons butter
6 tablespoons brown sugar
1/4 cup orange juice
1/2 teaspoon canela (or 1/4 teaspoon cinnamon)
1/4 teaspoon almond extract
6 small bananas, peeled and sliced
1/4 cup toasted pecans, chopped

Melt butter in a skillet over medium heat and add brown sugar, stirring until sugar is melted and bubbly. Add orange juice, canela and almond extract. Combine bananas and pecans with sugar mixture and stir 1 minute. Transfer to a bowl and serve warm or at room temperature.

Strawberry Filling:
2 pints strawberries, washed and hulled
Light brown sugar to taste
2 tablespoons orange liqueur, tequila, or rum

Slice strawberries and combine with brown sugar and liqueur in a small bowl. Mash slightly; allow to sit at room temperature 30 minutes to macerate.

White Chocolate:
4 ounces white chocolate, shaved with vegetable
**   peeler or coarsely chopped**

To assemble crêpes: Guests can top crêpes with several spoonfuls of banana or strawberry filling, roll into burritos, and add a sprinkle of white chocolate.

Perfect Picnics

A Backpacker's Picnic

Ginger-Nut Trail Mix • Roasted Eggplant and

Goat Cheese-Stuffed Bread Bowls • Frozen Strawberry

Yogurt Smoothies • Apricot-Piñon Oatmeal Bars

A Tailgating Party

Cheddar and Cayenne Crackers • Chilled Cantaloupe and

Champagne Soup • Blue Cheese-Stuffed Chicken Breasts with Roasted

Red Pepper Sauce • Red Wine-Marinated Cold Filet of Beef • Red Potato and

Crisp Vegetable Salad with Lemon-Dill Dressing • Orange-Almond

Cake with Fresh Fruit Salsa

A Riverside Picnic

New Mexico Blue-Corn Cups with Black Bean and

Corn Salsa • Chardonnay-Poached Salmon Fillets with

Smoky Chipotle Sauce • Gorgonzola and Green Bean Salad with

Mustard Vinaigrette • Red Beefsteak and Yellow Tomatoes in Fragrant Basil Oil • Chunky

Fruit Kebobs with Apple-Lime-Ginger and Apricot-Rum Glazes

Picnics are a favorite American activity. In Santa Fe, summer picnics are particularly glorious because of the dazzling blue skies, perfect weather and dramatic scenery right in our backyards.

Santa Feans are an outdoorsy bunch—even the most staid office workers will slip off their ties or shoes for the lunch hour and have a makeshift picnic on the nearest grassy patch. Most locals have a few favorite hikes that they do at least a couple of times weekly, and in the summer months these areas of scenic beauty sport picnic blankets galore.

Beautiful Atalaya Mountain is just a few miles east of the Plaza, and it is one of the locals' favorites. There, hikers can follow piñon-lined dirt paths to a 9,200-foot peak that offers an astounding view of Santa Fe and its mountainous backdrops. To the northeast is the Santa Fe Ski Area, where trails accessible from Hyde Park Road branch off into intimate clearings perfect for picnics. At the ski area itself, the ski lift operates for part of the summer and ascends to spectacular views of the area. There are some beautiful parks in town, some of which are equipped with picnic tables for easy setup.

For out-of-town picnics, head west to Bandelier National Monument, a verdant expanse of wilderness with spectacular ancient cliff dwellings and ruins plus miles of trails to suit every level of hiker. Charming Chimayo with its famous Santuario de Chimayo is less than an hour's drive northeast of the Plaza. The Santuario draws hundreds of pilgrims each year, particularly at Easter, when local worshippers—some carrying wooden crosses—walk the winding hilly route for days to reach the holy site. Excellent fly-fishing, pristine wilderness and endless picnic sites can be found in the scenic Pecos area. Or drive south and see Madrid, a former mining town full of shops and galleries housed in Victorian cottages.

Picnicking options in Santa Fe continue into the evening hours. For a nighttime picnic event Santa Fe style, join the locals at the tailgating parties held in the Opera's parking lot located on the road to Taos. For enthusiastic opera-goers, tailgating—or picnicking out of the back of your car—started as a matter of necessity; it is difficult to eat at a local restaurant, join the traffic up the opera's driveway, park and be on time for the performance. So, creative Santa Feans turned the opera tailgate into a local institution. Sometimes the costumes seen in the parking lot rival those that appear on stage. Tailgating menus range from simple to elaborate; those in black tie may serve a meal to match their attire while the more comfortably clad may choose soup and sandwiches. No matter the menu, the mountains are beautiful in the setting sun, and the opera remains one of The City Different's greatest cultural experiences.

The ideal setting awaits you no matter which direction you choose. Take along some of the following foods to make the day picture- and picnic-perfect.

A Backpacker's Picnic

You don't have to hike to the top of a mountain to find a beautiful spot for a picnic. Some of

the area's parking lots have views so dramatic that you may want to spread it out on the hood

of your car! A Backpacker's Picnic features excellent sandwiches with local cheese and vege-

tables. The frozen smoothies will keep the sandwiches cool and fresh in your backpack. Piñon

nuts are featured in the apricot bars in honor of New Mexico's state tree.

Ginger-Nut Trail Mix

This crunchy concoction has it all—chewy texture and rich nutty flavors with the unexpected bite of crystallized ginger. It's an easy-to-make gourmet snack for hikers to munch along the trail.

Yield: 5 cups

2 cups shelled, roasted and unsalted peanuts

1 cup roasted and unsalted pepitas (see p. 20)
1 cup roasted whole unblanched almonds
1 cup chopped crystallized ginger
2 teaspoons coarse salt
1 teaspoon white pepper

Combine all ingredients and toss to mix. Pack into individual plastic bags.

Roasted Eggplant and Goat Cheese-Stuffed Bread Bowls

The robust flavor of roasted vegetables blends perfectly with mild New Mexico goat cheese and tangy tomato topping in this vegetarian sandwich.

Yield: 6 servings
Vegetables:
1 Italian eggplant, about 1-1/4 pounds (or 4 to 5 Japanese eggplants)
2 small red bell peppers, roasted, peeled and sliced (see pp. 26, 13)
1 medium white onion, sliced into 1/4-inch-thick rounds
3 tablespoons olive oil
1 tablespoon lemon juice
1 tablespoon minced fresh oregano
Salt and freshly ground pepper
6 (4- to 5-inch-round) hard-crusted rolls
12 ounces goat cheese

Peel eggplant and cut into 1/4-inch-thick rounds. Heat oven to 400 degrees F. Mix olive oil, lemon juice and oregano together; brush on both sides of eggplant rounds. Lay eggplant slices in a single layer on a heavy baking sheet and roast about 20 minutes, turning once, or until tender and golden. Season to taste with salt and freshly ground black pepper. (Eggplant slices can also be grilled on the barbecue.) Cut slices crosswise into halves. Heat oven to 400 degrees F. Brush a roasting pan with 1 tablespoon olive oil and place onions in pan, tossing to coat with oil. Sprinkle with salt and pepper. Roast 15 minutes, uncovered. Stir and continue to roast another 15 minutes, or until onions are soft and slightly caramelized.

Note: If eggplant tastes bitter prior to cooking, arrange eggplant slices on several layers of paper towels, salt heavily and cover with another layer of paper towels. Allow to stand 1 hour. Use a rolling pin to lightly squeeze out moisture. Brush off any excess salt before cooking.

Tomato Topping:
3 cloves roasted garlic
4 large Roma tomatoes, cored and diced

1/4 cup sliced scallions
2 tablespoons chopped flat-leaf parsley
2 tablespoons chopped fresh basil
1-1/2 tablespoons balsamic vinegar
1/2 teaspoon salt

Mix garlic, tomatoes, scallions, parsley, basil, vinegar and salt in a small bowl. Place in a plastic bag to transport. Pour off excess accumulated juices at serving time.

To assemble sandwiches: Cut tops off six 4- to 5-inch-round hard-crusted rolls and, using a fork, scoop out soft bread from insides and bottoms. Divide 12 ounces of goat cheese between the rolls and spread on insides. Fill rolls 3/4 full with layers of eggplant, roasted red peppers and onions. Replace roll tops; wrap tightly with plastic wrap. At serving time, remove tops of rolls and spoon on tomato topping.

Note: Vegetables can be roasted and refrigerated the day before the hike. Assemble sandwich bowls just prior to departure. If a grill is available on your hike, make these sandwiches on lightly grilled sourdough bread that has been drizzled with olive oil. Serve open-faced.

Frozen Strawberry Yogurt Smoothies

Is there anything more refreshing on warm summer days than fruit and yogurt? Although fresh fruit makes the ultimate smoothie, frozen berries will work as well. After the mixture is blended, put in water bottles and freeze overnight.

Yield: 6 servings
2 cups cleaned fresh or frozen strawberries
1 small banana, sliced
1 (16-ounce) carton low-fat plain or vanilla yogurt
2 cups orange juice

Place all ingredients in blender jar and blend until smooth. Pour into individual plastic water bottles, leaving a couple of inches headroom. Place in freezer until ready to pack for your hike.

Apricot-Piñon Oatmeal Bars

The enticing aroma of these fruit bars baking in your kitchen is reason enough to try this recipe! These bars make good travelers and fit easily into pockets or backpacks.

Yield: 24 small bars

1 cup all-purpose flour
1 teaspoon ground canela
**   (or 1/2 teaspoon ground cinnamon)**
1/2 teaspoon baking powder
1/4 teaspoon salt
3/4 cup unsalted butter, room temperature
3/4 cup packed light-brown sugar
1 large egg
1 teaspoon pure vanilla extract
1/2 teaspoon almond extract
2 cups old-fashioned oatmeal

1 cup dried apricots, coarsely chopped
1/2 cup toasted piñon nuts (see p. 26)

Preheat oven to 350 degrees F. Lightly butter a 13 x 9-inch baking pan. Sift together flour, canela, baking powder and salt. Set aside.

Using an electric mixer, beat the butter and brown sugar together until mixture is light in color and fluffy. Beat in egg, vanilla and almond extract. Add dry ingredients and beat until blended. Using a wooden spoon, stir in oatmeal, dried apricots and piñon nuts. Spread batter in prepared pan, using your fingers to press down if necessary. Bake about 25 minutes, or until edges begin to pull away from sides of pan. Allow to cool before cutting into squares. These bars freeze well.

Note: Dried fruits can be chopped easily by lightly oiling your knife or the blade of a food processor.

A Tailgating Party

July marks the start of the opera season, one of The City Different's biggest draws. And no matter what's on at the opera, one of the best shows is always in the parking lot. You'll see it all there—mountain men in western garb eating jerky, men and women in creative black tie chatting with cowboys in ten-gallon hats, couples in caftans dancing to tapes playing in their cars. Menus are as varied as the dress and attitudes of the attendees, ranging from the simple to the elaborate. This menu, easily served from a cooler and a thermos, is lavish in its variety of flavors and textures.

Cheddar and Cayenne Crackers

A perfect crunchy choice for snacking while setting up your picnic.

Yield: about 36 crackers

1/2 cup butter
2 cups grated sharp cheddar cheese
2 cups all-purpose flour, sifted
1 teaspoon cayenne pepper (or to taste)

Using an electric mixer, cream butter and cheese together until fluffy and light. Gradually blend in flour and cayenne pepper. Form dough into 2 logs and wrap with plastic wrap. Refrigerate dough 1 hour or overnight.

Preheat oven to 325 degrees F. Slice dough into 1/4-inch-thick rounds and place on an ungreased baking sheet. Bake 15 minutes or until golden brown. Cool on wire racks.

Note: For a zippy Southwest accent, roll the chilled logs in hot chile powder before baking. Baked crackers can be frozen up to 1 month.

Chilled Cantaloupe and Champagne Soup

Quality melons make all the difference in this sweet mellow soup. Fragrant cantaloupes from the Farmers' Market and a dry New Mexico champagne give this soup its sparkle.

Yield: 6 servings

1-1/2 cups champagne
4 cups cubed cantaloupe or honeydew
1/2 cup plain yogurt
1/2 cup sour cream
1 tablespoon chopped fresh mint
Salt and sugar to taste
1/4 cup chopped chives

Pour champagne into a small saucepan and heat until liquid boils. Remove from heat and cool. Purée cantaloupe, yogurt, sour cream and mint in a blender or food processor. Add cooled champagne and purée briefly. Season to taste with salt and sugar. Refrigerate until ice cold. Serve in cups or small bowls garnished with chopped chives.

Blue Cheese-Stuffed Chicken Breasts with Roasted Red Pepper Sauce

A hint of sumptuous blue cheese gives the chicken a subtle intricacy of flavors when combined with the sweet red pepper sauce. This chicken is quite versatile and can be served hot or cold, whole or sliced.

Yield: 6 servings

Blue Cheese Stuffing:
2 tablespoons minced shallots
2 cloves garlic, minced
2 teaspoons butter
1 tablespoon minced fresh thyme
1 tablespoon minced fresh basil
1 egg white
4 ounces blue cheese, crumbled
1/4 cup dry bread crumbs
Salt and pepper to taste

In a small skillet, sauté shallots and garlic in butter until soft but not brown; cool. Combine thyme, basil, egg white, blue cheese, bread crumbs, seasonings and shallot mixture.

Chicken:
3 whole boneless chicken breasts, halved and flattened to 1/4-inch thickness
Salt and pepper to taste
1/4 cup each flour and fine cornmeal, mixed
4 tablespoons butter
2 tablespoons olive oil

Preheat oven to 350 degrees F. Season each breast with salt and pepper. Divide cheese mixture between chicken breasts and spread evenly over half of each breast. Fold other half of chicken breast over cheese filling, press with fingers to seal; secure with wooden toothpicks. Dredge breasts in flour-cornmeal mixture.

Heat butter and olive oil in a large ovenproof skillet over medium-high heat. When butter and oil turn a light brown, add chicken breasts and brown 3 minutes on each side. Place skillet in oven and bake until chicken is cooked through, about 20 minutes. Remove toothpicks and serve with Roasted Red Pepper Sauce.

Roasted Red Pepper Sauce (about 1-1/2 cups):
2 tablespoons olive oil
1/4 cup chopped white onion
1 tablespoon minced garlic
1 teaspoon hot pepper sauce (or to taste)
1 teaspoon coarse salt
1 cup chicken or vegetable broth
1/4 cup sun-dried tomatoes, snipped with scissors into slivers
2 red bell peppers, roasted, peeled and seeded (see pp. 26, 13)

Heat oil in a small skillet over medium heat. Add onion and sauté until golden; add garlic and sauté 1 minute. Add pepper sauce, salt, broth and dried tomatoes. Bring to a boil, reduce heat, and simmer 10 minutes. Remove from heat and cool slightly. Coarsely chop roasted red bell peppers in food processor or blender. Add broth mixture and blend until sauce is coarsely textured. Serve warm or at room temperature.

Red Wine-Marinated Cold Filet of Beef

Cold filet of beef has long been a staple for elegant picnics. This tender cut of meat offers a wonderful main-course addition to the menu. Plus, the leftovers are great!

Yield: 6 servings

1 center-cut filet of beef (about 2-1/2 to 3 pounds), trimmed and tied

Marinade:
1/4 cup plus 1 tablespoon olive oil
1/4 cup red wine
1 teaspoon dried thyme

2 cloves garlic, chopped
Salt and pepper

Whisk 1/4 cup oil, wine, thyme and garlic together and pour over meat in a plastic food storage bag. Refrigerate 8 to 24 hours, turning occasionally.

Preheat oven to 400 degrees F. Heat remaining oil in a heavy ovenproof frying pan. Remove meat from marinade, pat dry, and season with salt and pepper. Sear meat on high heat on all sides. Transfer pan to oven and roast 20 to 25 minutes, turning frequently to brown evenly. Use an instant-read thermometer to check for doneness (120 degrees F = rare, 135 degrees F = medium, and 145 degrees F = well done). For best texture and flavor, allow filet to cool for at least 20 minutes or up to 24 hours before slicing thinly. (This allows the juices to flow back into the outer layers of meat.) Serve slices of filet with Roasted Red Pepper Sauce (see p. 94) or Smoky Chipotle Sauce (see p. 98).

Red Potato and Crisp Vegetable Salad with Lemon-Dill Dressing

This classic is redolent of the tastes of summer! Green vegetables add a crisp updated touch to this marvelous salad.

Yield: 6 to 8 servings

Potato and Vegetable Salad:
6 small red potatoes
6 asparagus spears
1 cup sugar-snap peas, strings removed
2 small zucchinis, stem ends removed, quartered
   lengthwise and cut in 1/4-inch slices
1 cup small cherry tomatoes
1 green pepper, seeded and julienned
1/2 small red onion, thinly sliced
1/2 cup imported black olives, pitted and halved

Scrub potatoes and put in top part of a steamer above a pan of boiling water. Cover and steam about 30 minutes, or until tender. Drain and cut into quarters. Add asparagus

to a large uncovered pot of boiling water and cook until crisp-tender. Drain and rinse immediately with cold water. Pat dry with paper towels and cut into pieces. Repeat boiling and draining process with snap peas. Combine all vegetables in a large bowl, add Lemon-Dill Dressing and toss well. Refrigerate up to 8 hours.

Lemon-Dill Dressing:
1 egg yolk
   (see p. 53 if using uncooked eggs in a recipe)
3 tablespoons crème fraiche or sour cream
3 tablespoons fresh lemon juice
1 teaspoon salt
1 teaspoon minced garlic
1 teaspoon hot pepper sauce
3 tablespoons grated Parmesan cheese
1 tablespoon chopped fresh dill
2 tablespoons chopped fresh parsley
1 cup olive oil

Combine egg yolk, crème fraiche, lemon juice, salt, garlic and pepper sauce. Stir in Parmesan cheese, dill and parsley. Slowly whisk in olive oil until blended.

Crème fraiche:
1 cup heavy cream (not ultrapasteurized)
2 tablespoons buttermilk

Combine cream and buttermilk in a glass bowl and whisk until well blended. Loosely cover container with plastic wrap, letting some air in. Leave in a warm place from 12 to 24 hours. Cream will thicken and have a tangy nutty taste. Stir, cover and refrigerate until ready to use. May be kept in a tightly sealed container 2 to 3 weeks in the refrigerator.

Note: In cooked dishes, crème fraiche is superior to commercial sour cream as it is less likely to curdle when used in a hot sauce. For a reduced-calorie version, substitute half-and-half for heavy cream.

Orange-Almond Cake with Fresh Fruit Salsa

This dense citrus cake topped with a beautiful confetti of fresh fruit is sublime. Serve with a snowy sprinkling of confectioners' sugar for a lovely presentation.

Yield: 8 to 10 servings

Orange-Almond Cake:
2 small oranges
1 lemon
1 cup flour
1 tablespoon baking powder
4 eggs, room temperature
1/2 teaspoon salt
1-1/2 cups sugar
6 ounces toasted almonds, ground
2-2/3 cups olive oil
Confectioners' sugar for garnish

Place oranges and lemon in a pan and cover with water. Simmer over medium heat 20 minutes. Drain and cool. Cut lemon in quarters, discarding pulp and seeds; reserve rind. Cut oranges in quarters and discard seeds.

Preheat oven to 350 degrees F. Grease bottom of a 10-inch springform pan and line with parchment or waxed paper. Place lemon rind and orange quarters in a food processor fitted with a metal blade. Process until finely chopped. Sift flour and baking powder into a bowl and set aside. Place eggs and salt in the bowl of an electric mixer and beat at medium speed until foamy. Gradually add sugar and beat on medium-high about 3 minutes, or until mixture is light-colored and fluffy. Fold in flour mixture, then add fruit, nuts and olive oil. Beat at low speed until just incorporated. Do not overbeat. Pour batter into prepared pan and bake 1 hour and 15 minutes, or until top is golden brown and springs back when lightly pressed. Remove from oven and cool on a rack. Release cake from pan and peel off paper liner. Serve wedges heavily dusted with confectioners' sugar and ringed with Fresh Fruit Salsa.

Fresh Fruit Salsa (about 2 cups):
1/2 cup chopped mango
1/2 cup chopped banana
1/2 cup raspberries
1/2 cup chopped orange segments, white membranes removed
2 teaspoons orange-juice concentrate
1 teaspoon fresh lemon juice
1/2 teaspoon vanilla

Mix all ingredients together in a bowl. Salsa can be kept for a day in the refrigerator.

Note: Fresh Fruit Salsa is also delicious spooned over rich vanilla ice cream or fruit sorbets.

A Riverside Picnic

The Santa Fe. The Rio Grande. The Chama. For centuries, these important rivers have been the life sources of northern New Mexico, and Santa Feans have spread out on their banks for summertime picnics. With this menu, all you'll need for the perfect riverside picnic are a few hungry friends and a shady tree.

New Mexico Blue-Corn Cups with Black Bean and Corn Salsa

Blue corn is very high in protein and is more intensely flavored than white or yellow corn. The nutty corn cups are the perfect partner for the salsa.

Yield: 24 cups

Blue Corn Cups:
3 tablespoons cold butter, diced
3 tablespoons cream cheese or Neufchatel cheese, cut into small pieces
1/2 cup blue cornmeal
1 cup unbleached all-purpose flour
1/2 teaspoon salt
3 tablespoons sour cream

Preheat oven to 350 degree F. Put cream cheese and butter in a medium bowl. Sift together blue cornmeal, flour and salt; sprinkle over cheese and butter. Using a pastry blender or 2 knives, cut flour in until mixture resembles coarse crumbs. Add sour cream and mix until just combined.

Form pastry into balls, using about 1-1/2 tablespoons pastry. Press each ball into a mini-muffin tin to form a cup. (Pastry will be crumbly but will come together when pressed down in the muffin tin.) Bake until lightly browned, about 25 minutes. When cool, remove pastry cups from muffin tins. Using a slotted spoon, fill cups with Black Bean and Corn Salsa just before serving. The baked pastry cups can be wrapped well and frozen for 3 weeks.

Black Bean and Corn Salsa (about 2-1/2 cups):
1/4 cup finely chopped red onion
1 teaspoon minced garlic
2 tablespoons coarsely chopped fresh cilantro
1/2 teaspoon Mexican oregano
2 jalapeño chiles, stemmed, seeded and diced
1/2 teaspoon freshly toasted and ground cumin seed
1/2 teaspoon freshly toasted and ground coriander seed
2 tablespoons cider vinegar
2 tablespoons honey
3/4 cup fresh or frozen small corn kernels, cooked until crisp-tender
1/2 cup red bell pepper, seeded and diced
3/4 cup cooked black beans, rinsed and well drained
Salt to taste

Place onion, garlic, cilantro, oregano, and chiles in a medium bowl and mix. Whisk cumin, coriander, vinegar and honey together in a small bowl until well blended. Add corn, red bell pepper and beans to onion mixture. Stir in vinegar mixture and add salt to taste. Let salsa sit at room temperature 30 minutes to combine flavors.

Chardonnay-Poached Salmon Fillets with Smoky Chipotle Sauce

Imagine the sweet sharp flavor of chipotles accenting buttery salmon simmered in white wine. If there is a grill at your picnic site, grill the salmon there instead of poaching it ahead of time.

Yield: 6 servings
Poaching Liquid:
2 cups Chardonnay
2 cups water
3 lemon slices
1 clove garlic
1/2 cup chopped celery with leaves
2 whole cloves
5 coriander seeds
5 peppercorns
1 bay leaf
3 sprigs fresh parsley (or 1/2 teaspoon dried parsley)
6 (6-ounce) salmon fillets, similar in thickness

Place all ingredients except salmon in a large deep skillet. Bring to a boil, reduce heat to low and simmer, uncovered, 5 minutes. Wrap salmon fillets in a single piece of cheesecloth and lower into poaching liquid. Cover pan and simmer on low heat about 5 minutes. Check for doneness and remove from liquid when desired level is reached. Serve hot, at room temperature, or chilled. Top each fillet with Smoky Chipotle Sauce.

Smoky Chipotle Sauce (about 1-3/4 cups):
1 cup mayonnaise
1/2 cup sour cream
3 tablespoons minced chipotles en adobo sauce (see p. 18)
1 tablespoon lime juice
2 tablespoons chopped cilantro
1/2 teaspoon salt

Combine all ingredients in a small bowl and mix until combined. Taste and adjust seasonings.

Gorgonzola and Green Bean Salad with Mustard Vinaigrette

One of summer's stars is the green bean, a vegetable that adds welcome crispness and color to any outdoor menu. The green bean's affinity for mustard is highlighted in this recipe.

Yield: 6 servings
Gorgonzola and Green Bean Salad:
2 pounds fresh thin green beans, washed, trimmed and cut into bite-sized pieces
4 ounces Gorgonzola cheese, crumbled
1/2 cup toasted pecan halves

Bring a large pot of salted water to a boil and add green beans. Cook until barely tender, about 4 minutes. Rinse under cold water and drain well. Refrigerate until serving time. A half hour before serving, add cheese and pecans and toss mixture with Mustard Vinaigrette.

Mustard Vinaigrette:
1/2 teaspoon coarse salt
1 tablespoon white wine vinegar
5 tablespoons olive, canola, or grapeseed oil
1 clove garlic, peeled and minced
2 teaspoons Dijon mustard
1 teaspoon minced flat-leaf parsley

In a small bowl, whisk salt and vinegar together. Add remaining ingredients and whisk until mixture thickens and is well blended. Taste and adjust seasonings. Allow dressing to sit for at least 10 minutes.

Red Beefsteak and Yellow Tomatoes in Fragrant Basil Oil

When the garden is colored with all kinds of tomatoes, it is time to make this simple dish that is as visually vibrant as it is flavorful.

Yield: 6 servings

Tomatoes:
2 large beefsteak tomatoes, sliced
2 large yellow tomatoes, sliced
1/2 cup imported black olives
2 tablespoons capers

Arrange tomatoes, alternating colors, on a platter in concentric circles. Distribute olives and capers around edges of platter. Drizzle with Fragrant Basil Oil at serving time.

Fragrant Basil Oil:
1/2 cup fresh basil leaves, packed
2 tablespoons coarsely chopped flat-leaf parsley
2 tablespoons cider vinegar
1/2 cup olive oil
2 teaspoons sugar
1/2 teaspoon kosher salt
Freshly ground pepper to taste

Place all ingredients in a blender or food processor and mix until smooth.

Chunky Fruit Kebobs with Apple-Lime-Ginger and Apricot-Rum Glazes

Fresh fruit makes for the ultimate summer dessert. Two glorious-tasting glazes are offered for mix-and-match culinary magic.

Yield: 6 servings

Chunky Fruit Kebobs:
4 cups assorted chunks of fruit (large seedless grapes, strawberries, pineapple, melons, kiwis, orange slices, tangerine slices, starfruit)

36 fresh mint leaves
12 (6-inch) wooden skewers

Trim fruit as necessary and cut into desired shapes. Thread chunks of fruit and mint leaves (3 leaves per skewer) onto skewers, alternating colors and shapes. Wrap with plastic wrap and refrigerate until serving time.

Note: Select firm fruits that will not darken upon sitting. Use tiny cookie cutters to cut melons into stars or other shapes. For an attractive presentation, stick ends of skewers into the curved side of a melon half covered with ivy leaves.

Apple-Lime-Ginger Glaze (1 cup):
1 cup apple jelly
2 tablespoons fresh lime juice
1 tablespoon grated fresh ginger

Heat jelly over low heat in a small glass bowl in the microwave or in a small saucepan on the stovetop until barely melted. Remove from heat and stir in lime juice and ginger until well blended. Place in covered container and refrigerate until served.

Apricot-Rum Glaze (1 cup):
1 cup apricot preserves
1 tablespoon rum or frozen orange-juice concentrate
1 tablespoon fresh lemon juice

Heat preserves over low heat in a small saucepan on the stovetop or in a small glass bowl in the microwave until barely melted. Press through a sieve and discard any solid pieces of apricots. Stir in rum and lemon juice. Place in a covered container and refrigerate until ready to serve.

To serve: Drizzle glazes over fruit kebobs just prior to serving. Or pour glazes into plastic squeeze bottles and let guests swirl them on kebobs as they eat.

Note: These glazes keep for several weeks in the refrigerator and can be used to bolster flavors in fruit compotes and to top crêpes, dessert waffles and ice cream.

Glorious Garden Brunches and Luncheons

A Summer Garden Brunch

Chile-Spiced Fruit Platter • Chicken-Apple Brunch Patties • New Mexico Green Chile and

Feta Bread • Jalapeño and Chipotle Deviled Eggs • Mexican Iced Coffee

A Garden Tour Brunch

Spicy Cold Tomato Soup • Cumin Bread Crisps • Chicken Cazuelas • Piquant Cucumbers • Vanilla

Cookie Towers with Mixed Fruits and Fluffy Champagne Cream

A Walking Tour Luncheon

Santa Fe Sangria • Tequila-Marinated Prawns on Crispy Corn Cakes with Grilled

Peppers, Mixed Field Greens and Cilantro-Lime Vinaigrette • Warm Cinnamon-Scented Fudge Cakes

A Celebration of Local Herbs and Flowers

Tortilla-Crusted Baked Corn and Cheese Chiles Rellenos • Herbed Bean Salad with

Raddichio and Sherry-Shallot Vinaigrette • Cantaloupe and Honeydew in

Rosemary Syrup • Daiquiri Mousse on Summer Flowers

Adobe walls acted as formal property boundaries and afforded protection against hostile raiders in the old days. The oldest houses in town were often centered on courtyards featuring gardens and wells so that families, their horses and their livestock would have enough food and water to wait out any crisis.

Today, many yards and courtyards have been transformed into magnificent gardens with edible elements. Early European settlers established orchards and planted fruit trees; apricots, pears, peaches and cherries all grow well in the Santa Fe area today. Herbs of the region—oregano, wild marjoram and yerba buena (wild mint), to name a few—were originally prized for their curative powers as well as their ability to flavor and enhance foods. Flower petals from nasturtiums, roses and violets are edible as well as colorful and often top local salads. From flower gardens to fruit, vegetable and herb gardens, the Santa Feans' love of the outdoors is evident in their passion for gardening and for entertaining, which also blooms in the summer months.

Santa Fe garden parties have a relaxed informal elegance. The dress code is always casual—jeans dressed up with locally crafted silver and turquoise jewelry are an appropriate choice for nearly every occasion. Table settings are also fashionably casual—a riot of colors with lush bouquets of dewy garden blossoms set atop brightly patterned tablecloths. Earthy adobe walls absorb and soften the strong Santa Fe light, throwing a romantic glow over the intimate garden gatherings. Honeysuckle blooms add to the sun-baked sweetness of the midday air, thick and warm before the afternoon showers. Hummingbirds skim by, lighting on flowers to gather nectar, and butterflies, attracted by the sweet elements of the meal, hover around the guests.

For brunch and outdoor lunches, food is often served on festive platters or in large bowls so guests can serve themselves. Further, the shared activity of passing and holding platters for neighbors lends a sense of communal spirit, an important element of any New Mexico get-together. Unique local pottery brightens up tables even on the most formal of occasions (traditional china and crystal are rarely seen in Santa Fe). Some foods are served in artisan-crafted gourds, adding interesting shapes and textures to the table service. Locally-crafted cutlery—some pieces sporting turquoise or other semi-precious stones—make each Santa Fe table a unique work of art.

Sweet dishes are often served within a menu to balance the heat of chile-spiced foods. Pitchers of luscious sangria made from local wines and laden with fresh fruit are served over ice as an alternative to nonalcoholic beverages.

Santa Fe's beloved gardens provide the ultimate private settings for brunch and lunch gatherings. Join us in celebrating the bounty and beauty of our glorious Santa Fe gardens.

A Summer Garden Brunch

There is no setting more tranquil and secluded for brunch than a walled Santa Fe garden. The vivid blue sky, the velvety warm air, and the fragrant flowers all vie for attention with a perfectly planned menu. Colorful bouquets of cosmos, sunflowers, lavender and zinnias are set on tables to complete the Santa Fe ambiance.

1 tablespoon hot red chile powder
1 teaspoon sugar

Arrange fruit, jicama, and lime slices decoratively on a rimmed platter. Squeeze the halved lime over the jicama and fruit. Cover and refrigerate until serving time. Combine salt, chile powder and sugar in a small salt shaker.

Chicken-Apple Brunch Patties

Chicken and apples are a winning combination in these herbed sausages. Sage and cilantro add bright woodsy tones.

Yield: 6 to 8 servings

8 ounces boneless, skinless chicken or turkey breast, cut into small cubes
6 tablespoons butter, room temperature
1 tablespoon chopped garlic
1 tablespoon chopped cilantro
1 teaspoon chopped fresh sage
1 teaspoon chopped fresh oregano (or 1/2 teaspoon dried Mexican oregano)
1 tablespoon chile powder (mild, medium, or hot)
1/4 cup apple cider
1 cup tart apple, peeled and very finely diced
Salt to taste
Vegetable oil

Chile-Spiced Fruit Platter

This selection of fruits is fired with seasoned chile salt. Have a few shakers on hand so guests can add as much heat to the sweet as they like.

Yield: 6 to 8 servings

2 large oranges, peeled, sliced and seeded
1 large pink grapefruit, peeled, sliced and seeded
1 small pineapple, peeled, cored and sliced
1 (1-pound) jicama, peeled, sliced and cut into 1/4-inch-thick sticks
2 limes—1 sliced thin, 1 halved
1 tablespoon salt

Place first 8 ingredients in the bowl of a food processor and, using the metal blade, process to a coarse texture. Transfer mixture to a bowl and stir in diced apple. Refrigerate at least 1 hour for ease in handling.

Form meat mixture into 3-inch-diameter patties. In a heavy skillet, heat enough oil to coat the bottom. Fry the patties until cooked thoroughly and well browned. You may need to add additional butter to the skillet as the patties fry.

Note: The meat mixture can be prepared ahead, omitting the apple, and frozen. After defrosting, add the diced apple just before forming into patties.

New Mexico Green Chile and Feta Bread

Green chile and cheese marry well in this hearty loaf that could serve as a meal in itself.

Yield: 8 thick slices

1 (1-pound) loaf frozen bread dough, white or whole wheat, thawed overnight in refrigerator
2 teaspoons olive oil
1/2 cup chopped white onion
2 cloves garlic, minced
Cornmeal
1 cup crumbled mild feta or ricotta salata cheese
1/4 cup cream cheese
1/4 cup oil-packed, sun-dried tomatoes, drained and chopped
1 teaspoon dried Mexican oregano
1/2 teaspoon dried epazote (optional)
1/2 teaspoon salt
1 cup New Mexico chiles, roasted, peeled, seeded and chopped (well-drained frozen chiles can be substituted)
1 egg white
1/4 cup grated fresh Romano cheese

Heat oil in small skillet over medium heat and sauté onion until lightly browned. Add garlic and sauté for 1 minute. Roll thawed bread dough into a 16 x 10-inch rectangle on a surface lightly dusted with cornmeal. In a medium bowl, combine onion and garlic with all remaining ingredients except Romano cheese. Spread mixture over rolled-out dough, leaving a 1/2-inch border along all sides. Beginning with the long side, roll up dough, pinching along seam and ends to seal. Line a baking sheet with parchment paper (or coat with cooking oil) and place roll on it, seam side down. Cover with a towel and let rise in a warm place until doubled in size, about 1 hour.

Preheat oven to 350 degrees F. Sprinkle Romano cheese over top of roll. Bake 45 minutes, or until golden brown. Allow to cool 5 minutes before slicing.

CHEF'S CORNER: *It takes about five New Mexico green chiles to produce one cup of roasted, peeled and chopped chiles.*

3 jalapeño chiles, stemmed, seeded and
   finely diced
1 tablespoon chopped cilantro
1 tablespoon canned minced chipotles en adobo
   (see p. 18)

Place eggs in a saucepan large enough to hold eggs and
water to cover by 2 inches. Add 1 tablespoon salt to water.
Bring to a full rolling boil, turn heat to low, cover pan and
leave on heat 1 minute. Remove from heat and allow to
stand 15 minutes. Drain hot water from eggs; add ice
cubes and cold water to cover.

When eggs are cold, peel and cut in half lengthwise.
Transfer yolks to a bowl, and set aside the whites. Mash
yolks and 1-1/2 teaspoons salt with a fork. Blend in sour
cream, mayonnaise and scallions. Place half of yolk mixture
in another bowl. Add jalapeños and cilantro to one bowl
of yolks, chipotles en adobo to the other; mix. Fill reserved
egg whites with yolk mixtures. Cover and refrigerate until
ready to serve.

*Note: For a speedy recipe for deviled eggs, delete the jalapeño and
chipotle chiles and top each egg with chilled red caviar at serving time.*

Jalapeño and Chipotle Deviled Eggs

Herbs, jalapeños and chipotles liven the flavor of these
irresistible red-and-green deviled eggs, making them
brunch-table standouts.

Yield: 24 halves
12 large eggs
1 tablespoon plus 1-1/2 teaspoons salt
1/2 cup sour cream
1/4 cup mayonnaise
1/4 cup chopped scallions, white parts only

Mexican Iced Coffee

*This coffee's strength can be adjusted to individual tastes.
It's a refreshing frosty drink for a warm day and is easy to
transport for a pick-me-up on the road.*

Yield: about 16 cups
1/4 pound finely ground coffee
1 stick canela
3 tablespoons sugar (optional)

Mix coffee and canela with 2 cups water in a saucepan.
Stir well and bring to a boil. Remove from heat and allow
to stand 15 minutes. Strain through cloth or a paper coffee
filter into a saucepan. Add sugar and heat until boiling,
stirring to dissolve sugar. Cool and refrigerate until serving
time. For each serving, pour 2 tablespoons of coffee syrup
over ice and add milk, cold water, or cream to taste.

CHEF'S CORNER: *Eggs that are at
least a week old are easier to peel. Adding salt to the boiling water minimizes
the leakage from cracks in the eggs
while cooking.*

A Garden Tour Brunch

A local garden club holds a popular event over a few consecutive weekends each summer where participants can view some of the grandest private homes and gardens in Santa Fe. This brunch celebrates the bounty and beauty of such summer gardens.

Spicy Cold Tomato Soup

This delicious soup makes use of abundant best-of-the-summer tomatoes. It keeps several days in the refrigerator and is an excellent choice for a quick lunch.

Yield: 6 servings

1 cup chopped white onions
1 cup chopped celery hearts
2 tablespoons olive oil
7 large tomatoes, peeled and seeded (see p. 26)
3 cups tomato juice, chicken broth or
    vegetable broth
1 teaspoon chopped fresh oregano
    (or 1/2 teaspoon dried Mexican oregano)
1/2 teaspoon chopped fresh thyme
    (or 1/4 teaspoon dried thyme leaves)

1 tablespoon chile powder (mild, medium, or hot)
2 bay leaves
1 teaspoon sugar (more if tomatoes are acidic)
1 cup light cream
Salt and cayenne pepper to taste
Finely diced Roma tomatoes
Snipped chives

In a stockpot, sauté onions and celery in 2 tablespoons olive oil 5 minutes over medium-high heat. Add tomatoes, juice, herbs, chile powder, bay leaves and sugar; reduce heat to low and cook, stirring occasionally, until vegetables are soft, about 30 minutes. Remove bay leaves. Allow to cool slightly before placing in blender or food processor; process until a coarse purée is obtained. Do this in batches. Add cream and blend just enough to combine; season with salt and pepper. Chill in refrigerator. Garnish each serving with diced tomatoes and chives.

Note: Experiment with other herbs from your garden. Also, whole milk, half-and-half or chicken broth can be substituted for cream.

Cumin Bread Crisps

These bread crisps make great snacks, as well as being the perfect crunchy accompaniment to the creamy chilled tomato soup.

Yield: 16 slices

3 tablespoons melted butter
2 eggs
1 tablespoon olive oil
1 teaspoon whole toasted cumin seeds,
**   lightly crushed**
1/2 teaspoon freshly toasted and ground coriander
1 teaspoon salt
1/2 teaspoon coarsely ground pepper
**   (use an aromatic, good-quality pepper)**
16 slices crusty 3-inch-diameter French bread,
**   cut 1/2-inch thick**

Preheat oven to 400 degrees F. Coat a rimmed baking sheet with butter. Beat eggs and oil together; combine with spices in a small flat dish. Dip bread slices on both sides in egg mixture. Shake off any excess and coat each side in spice mixture. Place slices of bread in a single layer on baking sheet; bake 10 to 15 minutes, turning once, or until golden brown. Once completely cool, these crisps keep well in an airtight container or in the freezer. They can be served at room temperature or reheated.

Chicken Cazuelas

A cazuela is a clay cooking pot used in Mexico. Earthenware cazuelas impart a rustic flavor to foods, but glass casserole dishes used in this recipe substitute nicely. These mini-casseroles offer an appealing combination of flavors with their light, soufflé-like crusts topping a flavorful chicken mixture.

Yield: 8 servings

4 cups cooked chicken or turkey, cubed and
**   salted to taste**
1 teaspoon dried Mexican oregano

1 cup roasted, peeled and chopped green chiles
**   (well-drained frozen chiles can be substituted)**
1/4 cup sliced green or black olives
1 cup shredded sharp cheddar cheese, divided
1 cup shredded Monterey Jack cheese, divided
1/4 cup flour
1-1/2 cups milk
4 large eggs, separated
2 teaspoons chile powder
1 teaspoon salt

Preheat oven to 325 degrees F. Place chicken in 8 well-buttered individual casserole dishes or a 9 x 13-inch baking dish. Mix oregano, chiles and olives together and distribute evenly over chicken. Mix together 3/4 cup of each cheese and sprinkle over chicken. Place flour in a small bowl and gradually whisk in milk until smooth. Whisk in egg yolks, chile powder and salt. Using an electric mixer, beat egg whites until they hold stiff peaks. Fold egg whites into yolk mixture and spread evenly over chicken. Sprinkle tops of casseroles with remaining cheeses. Bake casseroles until tops are well browned, about 30 minutes. (An extra 15 minutes of baking time will be necessary for a large casserole.) Let stand a few minutes before serving.

Piquant Cucumbers

These cucumbers are cool and refreshing palate pleasers served alongside the hearty casseroles. For an appealing presentation, serve on a bed of cilantro or watercress leaves and sprinkle the rim of the serving plate with chile powder.

Yield: 6 servings

3/4 cup white vinegar
1/3 cup sugar
1 teaspoon chile caribe (see p. 18)
**   or hot red pepper flakes**
1/2 teaspoon coarse salt
2 pounds long European-style cucumbers
1/4 cup finely chopped red onions
2 jalapeños, seeded and chopped

Combine vinegar, sugar, chile caribe and salt in a large bowl. Stir until sugar is completely dissolved. Wash cucumbers well, score with a fork, cut into 1/4-inch-thick slices, then cut into halves. Add cucumbers, onions and jalapeños to vinegar mixture. Cover and refrigerate up to 4 hours, stirring occasionally. Use tongs or a slotted spoon to serve.

Vanilla Cookie Towers with Mixed Fruits and Fluffy Champagne Cream

This is a delightful stacked dessert featuring thin vanilla cookies and raspberry-flavored fruits topped with clouds of champagne cream.

Yield: 6 servings

Vanilla Cookie Towers:

6 egg whites

1 cup plus 2 tablespoons superfine sugar

3/4 cup unsalted butter, melted and cooled to room temperature

1/2 teaspoon vanilla extract

1/2 teaspoon almond extract

1 cup plus 2 tablespoons sifted flour

Preheat oven to 350 degrees F. Line baking sheet with parchment paper. Beat egg whites and sugar together until smooth. Add melted butter and extracts, then spoon flour over top of mixture and lightly fold it in. Place 12 tablespoons of batter on lined baking sheet, spacing well apart. Spread each spoonful into a 4-inch circle. Bake until very lightly browned, about 7 minutes. Cool on baking sheet, then carefully remove with a thin spatula. Store in airtight container until ready to use.

Mixed Fruits:

3 cups cleaned and sliced mixed fruit (strawberries, raspberries, blueberries, blackberries, mangoes, peaches, kiwis or nectarines)

6 tablespoons raspberry jam, strained

Mix jam with fruit and allow to sit at room temperature 30 minutes.

Note: For a hot and zingy fruit filling, add 2 teaspoons chipotle chile powder to raspberry jam.

Fluffy Champagne Cream:

3 egg yolks	**1/2 cup champagne**
1/4 cup sugar	**1/2 cup heavy cream**
Pinch of salt	

Combine all ingredients except cream in the top of a double boiler. Place over simmering water and whisk vigorously until mixture thickens and is pale yellow. Remove from heat and place in a large bowl filled with ice. Whisk until cold. Whip cream to soft peaks and fold into egg mixture. Refrigerate until serving time.

To assemble: Place a cookie on each dessert plate and spoon on about 1/2 cup of fruit. Top with a spoonful of Fluffy Champagne Cream. Repeat layering, using remaining cookies, fruit and cream. Allow desserts to sitfor a few minutes so that cookies will absorb fruit juices and soften somewhat.

A Walking Tour Luncheon

Numerous walking tours of Santa Fe are offered during the summer. They are a great way to learn more about the city's vibrant history and to get to know your way around town. After a morning tour of the city's renowned sights, visitors and locals alike enjoy relaxing in an exquisite garden for lunch.

Heat sugar and water together, stirring to a boil. Continue boiling over medium heat 2 minutes. Cool. Combine all ingredients except champagne or soda water and chill. Serve sangria mixture over ice, adding about 1/4-cup champagne or soda water to each glass as it is served.

Santa Fe Sangria

Along with wine, good sangria features lots of fresh fruit and an element of fizz. For an interesting variation, make white sangria by substituting white wine for the red wine and apple juice for the orange juice.

Yield: 12 servings

1/2 cup sugar
1/2 cup water
2 bottles red wine
1 red apple, unpeeled and thinly sliced
2 peaches, peeled and thinly sliced
1 orange, unpeeled and thinly sliced
1 lemon, unpeeled and thinly sliced
1 cup freshly squeezed orange juice
1 bottle champagne or soda water

Tequila-Marinated Prawns on Crispy Corn Cakes with Grilled Peppers, Mixed Field Greens and Cilantro-Lime Vinaigrette

This crowd-pleasing dish explodes with a variety of flavors and textures. Tequila in the marinade adds an edge that balances the richness of the prawns. The corn cakes are also a delicious side dish for any grilled poultry or meat.

Yield: 6 servings

18 prawns or jumbo shrimp, shelled and deveined

Marinade:
1 cup tequila
1 tablespoon Asian red chili paste
3 tablespoons olive oil
1/4 cup chopped white onion
2 cloves garlic, minced
1/2 cup freshly squeezed lime juice
Salt and pepper to taste

Mix all ingredients in a glass bowl. Add prawns and marinate about 15 minutes. Drain and grill 3 to 4 minutes on each side.

Crispy Corn Cakes:
1 cup all-purpose flour
2/3 cup yellow cornmeal
1 teaspoon baking soda
3 eggs
3/4 cup whole milk
2 tablespoons butter, melted and cooled
2 tablespoons chopped cilantro
2 jalapeño chiles, seeded and diced
1/4 cup sliced scallions, including some green tops
1 teaspoon salt
1 teaspoon cayenne pepper
Melted butter

Combine all ingredients except melted butter in a bowl, stirring by hand until well combined. Cover and let stand at room temperature 30 minutes. Heat a large sauté pan over medium heat and brush lightly with melted butter. Ladle batter into pan, creating eighteen 3-inch-diameter cakes. Cook until lightly browned on bottom. Flip cakes and cook until second side is brown. Make remaining cakes in same manner, brushing pan with butter as needed. (Corn cakes can be cooked up to 1 hour ahead of serving and kept warm in a 250-degree F oven.)

Grilled Peppers:
1 yellow bell pepper
1 red bell pepper
1 poblano chile
Roast, peel and seed peppers (see pp. 26, 13); cut into strips and set aside to drain on paper towels.

Field Greens:
6 cups mixed, lively flavored field greens
(raddichio, arugula, watercress, curly
endive or baby field greens), cleaned

To serve: Arrange greens on 6 plates. Place 3 corn cakes in center of each plate. Top with prawns and garnish with grilled peppers around edges of plates. Drizzle generously with Cilantro-Lime Vinaigrette.

Cilantro-Lime Vinaigrette:
1/4 cup fresh lime juice
5 tablespoons apple cider vinegar
1/2 cup rice wine vinegar
3/4 cup olive oil
1 tablespoon minced cilantro leaves
1/4 cup honey
1 teaspoon Dijon mustard
Pinch of cayenne chile powder
Salt and pepper to taste

Whisk all ingredients together in a small bowl. Taste and adjust seasonings.

Warm Cinnamon-Scented Fudge Cakes

These outrageously delicious cakes have creamy rich centers that are appealing to true chocolate lovers. To gild the lily further, top cakes with tiny scoops of rich vanilla ice cream made with a melon-baller.

Yield: 6 cakes

Cocoa powder
6 ounces bittersweet chocolate,
    coarsely chopped
2 sticks unsalted butter,
    cut into slices
3 large eggs, room temperature
3 large egg yolks,
    room temperature
1/4 cup sugar
2 teaspoons ground canela
    (or 1 teaspoon cinnamon)
1/3 cup all-purpose flour
 Confectioners' sugar

Preheat oven to 400 degrees F. Lightly butter insides of six 3-1/2-inch-diameter ramekins. Dust with cocoa and shake out any excess. Set in a baking pan. Using a microwave (about 2 minutes on low temperature) or double boiler, melt chocolate, stirring occasionally. Remove from heat, add butter and stir until smooth. Cool.

Using an electric mixer, beat eggs, egg yolks and sugar until pale yellow in color. On low speed, blend in cooled chocolate mixture and canela. Fold the flour into the chocolate-egg mixture with a rubber spatula. Divide the batter evenly among the prepared ramekins. Bake 14 minutes, or until cakes are set on top. Remove from oven and let stand about 3 minutes. Run a sharp,

thin knife around insides of ramekins to loosen each cake. Place warm cakes on plates that have been liberally dusted with confectioners' sugar. Using a small sieve, dust tops of cakes lightly with confectioners' sugar.

Note: Prepare ramekins and ingredients ahead of time to minimize last-minute preparation.

A Celebration of Local Herbs and Flowers

There's something wonderful about growing herbs and flowers and using them to complement a meal. They please the senses with their beauty, their delicate scents and their variety of flavors. This lunch or light dinner is a celebration of seasonal and regional specialties accented with herbs and flowers.

Tortilla-Crusted Baked Corn and Cheese Chile Rellenos

These baked rellenos with a crunchy coating offer a new approach to the traditional deep-fried rellenos. The corn-and-herb filling adds a sweet note to the dish.

Yield: 6 servings

1 cup roasted corn kernels, about 1 large ear (see p. 25)
1/4 cup crumbled goat cheese
1/4 cup grated asadero or Monterey Jack cheese
3 scallions, trimmed and sliced
1/4 cup finely chopped fresh cilantro or flat-leaf parsley
1 clove garlic, minced
1/2 teaspoon dried epazote (optional)
Salt and freshly ground pepper to taste
6 Anaheim, New Mexico green or poblano chiles, roasted and peeled
3 egg whites, lightly beaten
1 cup flour
1 cup dry bread crumbs
1/2 cup finely crushed tortilla chips
Cilantro sprigs
Finely diced tomatoes

Preheat oven to 400 degrees F. Mix together corn, cheeses, scallions, cilantro, garlic, epazote, salt and pepper. Taste and adjust seasoning.

Make a 2-inch-lengthwise cut into flesh of each chile and, using the tip of a spoon, scrape out core and seeds, leaving body of chile and stem intact. Stuff each chile lightly with cheese mixture. Place flour on a plate and egg whites in a shallow bowl; mix bread crumbs and crushed tortilla chips together on another plate. Dip each chile first in flour, then in egg whites, then in crumb mixture. Place chiles on a greased baking sheet and spray tops generously with vegetable cooking spray. Bake until lightly browned, about 20 minutes. Garnish with sprigs of cilantro and diced tomatoes.

CHEF'S CORNER: *Roasted and stuffed green chiles can be refrigerated 24 hours or frozen up to three months. Allow chiles to reach room temperature before final breading and baking.*

Herbed Bean Salad with Raddichio and Sherry-Shallot Vinaigrette

Any variety of garden-fresh herbs can be used to accent this updated three-bean salad.

Yield: 6 servings

Bean Salad:
1 cup cooked kidney beans
1 cup cooked black beans
1 cup cooked small white beans
1/2 cup diced red onion
1/2 cup finely chopped celery
1 green pepper, diced
1/4 cup oil-packed sun-dried tomatoes, drained and chopped
2 tablespoons chopped mixed fresh herbs (chives, cilantro, thyme, parsley, rosemary, sage or marjoram)
1 small head raddichio, shredded

In a large bowl, toss all ingredients except raddichio with vinaigrette. Refrigerate up to 8 hours to allow bean mixture to absorb marinade. Stir in raddichio just before serving.

Vinaigrette:
1/3 cup extra virgin olive oil, divided
2 shallots, minced
2 cloves garlic, minced
1/2 cup sherry vinegar, divided
1 teaspoon brown sugar
1/2 cup apple or orange juice
Pinch of cayenne pepper
Coarse salt to taste

Heat 1 tablespoon olive oil in a small skillet. Add shallots and garlic; sauté until just softened. Add half the vinegar and boil until reduced by half. Add rest of vinegar, olive oil and remaining ingredients; simmer 2 minutes. Cool to lukewarm before using.

Note: If using canned beans, be sure they are a top-quality brand, drained and well rinsed. Try making this salad with dried beans that have been soaked and cooked; preparation time will take longer, but the salad will have a terrific taste and texture.

Cantaloupe and Honeydew in Rosemary Syrup

Newly harvested melons come to Santa Fe markets in August. The rosemary syrup infuses the melons with a subtle herbaceous scent and flavor.

Yield: 6 servings

3/4 cup sugar
3/4 cup white wine
1 teaspoon grated lime peel
1 tablespoon chopped fresh rosemary leaves
2 teaspoons whole black peppercorns, lightly crushed
6 tablespoons fresh orange juice
1/4 cup fresh lime juice
3 cups honeydew, cut in 2-inch cubes
3 cups cantaloupe, cut in 2-inch cubes

In a small saucepan, stir together all ingredients except melons. Bring mixture to a boil; simmer 5 minutes. Chill until cold. Strain syrup through a fine sieve, pressing hard on solids. Toss melon cubes with syrup up to 4 hours before serving.

Daiquiri Mousse on Summer Flowers

Serve this delicate mousse on a beautiful bed of edible flowers from your garden. Nasturtiums, violets, carnations, rose petals and herb blossoms all suggest shades of summer.

Yield: 14 servings

10 eggs, separated
2 cups sugar, divided
1/2 cup freshly squeezed lime juice
1/2 cup freshly squeezed lemon juice
Grated peels of 2 lemons and 2 limes
Pinch of salt
2 tablespoons unflavored gelatin
1/2 cup light rum
2-1/2 cups heavy cream, divided

Beat egg yolks until foamy. Gradually beat in 1 cup of sugar until mixture is smooth and pale yellow. Blend in juices, grated peels and salt. Place in a saucepan and cook over low heat, stirring constantly until thickened. Soften gelatin in rum and stir into hot custard to dissolve. Set aside until cool, stirring occasionally.

Lightly spray a 6-cup soufflé dish with vegetable oil; add a waxed-paper collar around the rim. Beat egg whites until stiff, then slowly add remaining cup of sugar. Beat until peaks form and mixture is stiff but not dry. Fold a large spoonful of cooled custard into egg whites, then fold egg whites into remaining custard. Whip 2 cups of heavy cream and fold into mixture. Spoon into soufflé dish and refrigerate overnight. At serving time, whip remaining 1/2 cup of heavy cream, remove paper collar, and ice top of mousse with whipped cream. Arrange handfuls of edible flowers on dessert plates and place spoonfuls of mousse on top.

Santa Fe's Starry Nights

A Supper Under the Portal

Gazpacho Salad • Sirloin Tips with Poblanos and Tomatoes • Warm

Flour Tortillas • Chile and Red Pepper Strips • Cilantro Rice with Toasted

Piñon Nuts • Creamy Espresso Parfaits

A Dinner Celebrating Musical Santa Fe

Red Oakleaf Lettuce with Peppered Pears, Honey-Sherry Vinaigrette and Toasted

Walnuts • Roast Pork with Ancho-Cherry Glaze • Herb and Scallion Polenta Spoonbread • Sauté of

Baby Summer Vegetables • Apple Tart in Phyllo Crust with Warm Cajeta Sauce

A Stargazers' Cookout

Seasonal Mixed Greens with Balsamic Dressing • Chile-Barbecued Salmon with Jalapeño,

Herb and Orange Relish • Oven-Roasted Corn with Chipotle Aioli and Tomato-Basil Butter • Rosy Wine and

Raspberry-Poached Peaches • A Constellation of Chocolate-Dipped Fruits

Is there anything more enchanting than dining outside in the refreshingly cool mountain air under a clear starry sky?

On summer nights, locals often entertain under the portal, an outdoor living space akin to a covered patio. Classic portals are constructed of posts supporting a roof made of *vigas* (log beams) and *latillas* (slim poles). Providers of shade and shelter, portals today are usually treated as an outdoor extension of a living room. Tables and chairs for dining, benches and chaises for lounging and reading, lush potted trees and plants, and baskets and pots typically make up the decor. Many portals also feature a fireplace, an essential feature to hold the chill at bay as summer nights in Santa Fe are often cool and breezy; temperatures can be a good 20 to 30 degrees below daytime highs. Outdoor fireplaces also lend a cozy charm to gatherings. When the sun goes down, Santa Feans love to gather around the crackling fires that fill the nighttime sky with the intoxicating scent of piñon.

Astronomy and gastronomy are two sciences that are especially well suited to each other. Fresh air and starlight are known to enhance the appetite, and stargazing is an activity best enjoyed after an excellent meal. The nighttime skies over The City Different are well worth the attention. Some constellations are so vivid from the city's 7,000-foot elevation that they look like diamond-paved roadways.

If you can tear your gaze from the heavens, Santa Fe offers a galaxy of evening cultural events to explore. Music, theater and dance are an important part of life here, and there are an abundance of seasonal performances. In addition to the Santa Fe Opera, there are classical and contemporary musical events, ranging from chamber music choirs to mariachi bands. A world-renowned flamenco troupe spends its summers in Santa Fe and tours the world for the remainder of the year. Born in southern Spain, flamenco has long been a part of the Santa Fe scene; the six-stringed Spanish guitar produces music as dramatic as the flamenco dancers' precise movements. The Plaza, the heart of the city, has musicians gracing its bandstand for concerts during much of the summer.

Theater, too, is alive and well in Santa Fe. Professional theater groups perform plays by emerging and established playwrights. Other local groups produce melodramas for such special occasions as the Fiestas de Santa Fe. Many touring dance groups visit the area, contributing their energy to the cultural mix of events.

Santa Fe's starry nights provide a magical setting that dazzle both locals and visitors alike.

A Supper Under the Portal

The portal is far more than a pretty architectural feature of adobe houses. Santa Feans use their portals as outdoor living space for much of the year. In the spring, they provide shelter against sudden snowstorms; in the summer and fall, portals are shady, cozy venues for lounging and entertaining. This menu is characteristic of a casual summer supper shared with friends under the portal.

Gazpacho Salad

Familiar gazpacho soup ingredients come together in a refreshing and appealing salad. Improvise by adding your favorite fresh vegetables and herbs.

Yield: 6 servings

Gazpacho Salad Dressing:
1/2 cup vegetable or olive oil
1/4 to 1/2 cup red wine vinegar (depending upon acidity)
2 large cloves garlic, minced
1 tablespoon minced cilantro leaves
1 teaspoon chopped fresh oregano leaves
1/4 teaspoon toasted and ground cumin seeds
Salt and ground pepper to taste

Place dressing ingredients in a small jar and shake until well combined. (Use 1/4 cup vinegar to begin with, taste, then add more if needed.)

Gazpacho Salad:
1 unpeeled English seedless cucumber, cut into large dice (peel if using a regular cucumber)
1 green pepper, trimmed and cut into large dice
1 red pepper, trimmed and cut into large dice
2 jalapeño chiles, stemmed, seeded and sliced thinly
3 Roma tomatoes, cut into sixths
1 large avocado, diced
1/2 cup sliced black olives
1/4 cup finely chopped red onion
2 tablespoons chopped parsley
2 tablespoons chopped cilantro leaves
2 cups shredded romaine lettuce
1/2 cup crushed tortilla chips

In a large bowl, toss together all ingredients except lettuce and tortilla chips with enough dressing to moisten. Divide lettuce between individual salad plates, top with salad mixture, and sprinkle with tortilla chips just before serving.

Note: Except for avocado, salad ingredients can be prepared several hours ahead and placed in separate piles in the salad bowl. The dressing can also be made ahead, but don't toss the salad until serving time.

Sirloin Tips with Poblanos and Tomatoes

This basic recipe is as flavorful as it is easy to prepare. When made a day ahead, the flavors are even better. If you are going to reheat the meat, be sure not to overcook it when you are sautéing.

Yield: 6 servings

2 pounds tender, well-trimmed boneless beef (sirloin, sirloin tips, rib eye, or tenderloin)
Vegetable oil

1-1/2 medium white onions, halved and
    thinly sliced

2 tablespoons finely chopped garlic

9 Roma tomatoes, sliced (peeling is optional)

2 roasted, peeled and chopped poblano or
    New Mexico chiles

1 teaspoon dried Mexico oregano

1/4 teaspoon dried thyme

2 bay leaves

1-1/2 cups beef broth

Salt to taste

Cut meat into 3/4-inch cubes and dry on paper towels.
Add enough oil to a deep skillet to lightly coat the bottom;
bring to medium-high heat. Sauté meat in batches to
ensure proper browning and set aside. (This will take
4 to 5 minutes for medium-rare.)

Reduce heat to medium, add onions and sauté until softened and lightly browned. Add garlic and sauté 1 minute.
Add tomatoes and continue to cook 3 minutes, stirring
occasionally. Add remaining ingredients and simmer over
low heat 15 minutes, or until most of the liquid is gone.
Add meat with any accumulated juices and heat until meat
is warmed. Discard bay leaves and adjust seasonings.

Serve in shallow bowls with Warm Flour Tortillas, which
can be torn into bite-sized wrappers or used to soak up
the flavorful juices.

Warm Flour Tortillas
(see p. 24 for recipe and instructions)

Chile and Red Pepper Strips

These pepper strips can be served as a side dish or as an alternative to meat in Sirloin Tips with Poblanos and Tomatoes (see pp. 116–17). For a special vegetarian burrito, add a little crumbled salty white cheese and diced tomatoes to chiles and wrap in a warm tortilla.

Yield: 6 servings

6 poblano, New Mexico, or Anaheim chiles, roasted, peeled and seeded (see p. 13)
1 red bell pepper, roasted, peeled and seeded (see pp. 26, 13)
4 tablespoons olive oil
1 medium red onion, sliced 1/4-inch thick
2 large cloves roasted garlic, mashed
1 teaspoon mixed dried herbs (such as Mexican oregano, marjoram, or thyme)
1/2 cup heavy cream or crème fraiche (see p. 95)
1/4 cup chicken broth
Freshly ground black pepper
2 tablespoons sliced green scallion tops

Cut chiles and bell pepper into 1/2-inch strips and pat dry on paper towels. Heat oil in a large skillet over medium heat. Stirring frequently, sauté onions 5 to 6 minutes, or until they begin to brown. Stir in garlic, herbs, cream and broth; cook 5 minutes, or until liquid has thickened. Gently stir in chiles and bell pepper; heat 2 minutes. Sprinkle with black pepper and scallion tops.

Cilantro Rice with Toasted Piñon Nuts

The unexpected flavors of cilantro and toasted piñon nuts enliven this rice dish.

Yield: 6 to 8 servings

2-3/4 cups chicken broth
1/2 cup roughly chopped cilantro
1/4 cup lemon juice
1/2 teaspoon salt
1/2 teaspoon toasted and ground coriander (see p. 26)
2 tablespoons olive or vegetable oil
1-1/2 cups long-grain rice
1/2 cup chopped onion
1/4 cup lightly toasted piñon nuts (see p. 26)

Blend 1 cup chicken broth with cilantro in a food processor or blender. Combine mixture with remaining broth, lemon juice, salt and coriander in a large saucepan. Heat oil in a skillet and sauté rice and onion until rice is opaque and begins to turn golden brown. Bring broth to a boil, add

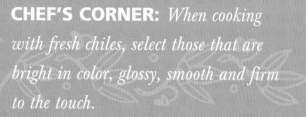

CHEF'S CORNER: *When cooking with fresh chiles, select those that are bright in color, glossy, smooth and firm to the touch.*

rice mixture, and reduce heat to low. Cover and cook 15 to 20 minutes, or until rice is tender and has absorbed all liquid. Remove from heat and let rice sit, covered, for 5 minutes more. Stir in nuts.

Note: Serve both rice and beans when feeding a crowd of people with big appetites (for Refried Black Beans, see p. 70).

Creamy Espresso Parfaits

Another wonderful way to enjoy coffee! With the intense flavors of crème de cacao and coffee liqueur, this luxurious dessert is a wonderful finalé to any dinner.

Yield: 6 servings

6 large egg yolks
   (see p. 53 if using uncooked eggs in recipes)

1-1/4 cups confectioners' sugar
1 scant tablespoon instant espresso coffee
1/2 teaspoon canela
2 tablespoons crème de cacao
2 cups heavy cream, whipped
1/4 cup coffee liqueur
18 chocolate-covered coffee beans

Using an electric mixer, beat egg yolks with sugar until thick and pale yellow. Mix in coffee, canela and crème de cacao. Using a rubber spatula, fold in whipped cream. Pour into 6 goblets and chill at least 5 hours. At serving time pour a little coffee liqueur over each parfait and set on a small serving plate. Place 3 chocolate-covered coffee beans at the base of each goblet.

A Dinner Celebrating Musical Santa Fe

Culture hits a high note with summer's many musical performances. In addition to the opera, Santa Fe boasts events ranging from classical orchestras to mariachi bands. A bit of fiery flamenco entertainment and a warm hearty meal are just the thing for Santa Fe's cool summer evenings.

Red Oakleaf Lettuce with Peppered Pears, Honey-Sherry Vinaigrette and Toasted Walnuts

This salad has numerous fantastic flavors to intrigue the palate. The combination of sweet and pungent pears with a mild loose-leaf lettuce and tangy dressing can't be beat.

Yield: 6 servings

Honey-Sherry Vinaigrette:
2 tablespoons honey
1 tablespoon Dijon mustard
3 tablespoons sherry vinegar
1/4 cup walnut oil
1/2 cup canola oil
Salt to taste

In a small bowl, mix honey, mustard and vinegar. Slowly whisk in oils and season with salt.

Salad:
6 cups cleaned and torn red oakleaf lettuce leaves
2 tablespoons snipped chives

Peppered Pears:
Freshly ground black pepper
2 ripe pears, peeled and sliced into thin wedges

Toasted Walnuts:
1/4 cup toasted walnuts, coarsely chopped
    (see p. 26)

Toss lettuce and chives with enough Honey-Sherry Vinaigrette to moisten; arrange on salad plates. Grind enough pepper to cover bottom of a small plate. Lightly roll peeled edges of pear slices in pepper and arrange on lettuce. Sprinkle salad with Toasted Walnuts.

Note: For an extravagant taste experience, sprinkle a little crumbled blue cheese over the top of each salad.

Roast Pork with Ancho-Cherry Glaze

Chokecherries grew abundantly at Anasazi sites in the area of Bandelier National Monument, and Spanish settlers used them to make special wines for religious events. This glaze, inspired by chokecherries, provides a sweet-hot crust that perfectly highlights the succulent pork roast.

Yield: 6 or more servings

Ancho Purée:
6 ancho chiles, stemmed and seeded
2 cups hot water

Preheat oven to 250 degrees F. Place chiles on baking sheet and roast 5 minutes, turning once. Watch carefully so that chiles do not blacken or burn. Transfer to a large bowl and cover with hot water. Place a plate on top of chiles to keep them submerged; let stand 30 minutes to soften. Transfer chiles to a blender, add enough soaking water to cover, and purée until smooth. Strain through a fine sieve, pressing hard on solids to extract chile purée. Save extra purée for another use.

Ancho-Cherry Glaze:
2 tablespoons olive oil
1 teaspoon finely chopped garlic
1/2 cup ancho purée
1 cup cherry jelly or plum jam
1 tablespoon fresh lemon juice
1/2 teaspoon ground allspice
1/2 teaspoon dried thyme
1/2 teaspoon salt
1/2 cup dried tart cherries, softened in
    a little hot water and drained

Heat olive oil in a medium frying pan and sauté garlic until lightly browned. Add ancho purée, jelly or jam, lemon juice, allspice, thyme and salt. Cook 3 minutes over low heat. Cool to room temperature in a nonreactive pan large enough to hold the pork roast. Remove 1/2 cup of glaze to a small bowl, mix with cherries, and refrigerate until serving time.

Roast Pork:
1 (3- to 4-pound) pork loin roast, bone-in

Place meat in pan with glaze, turn to coat well, cover and refrigerate 4 to 24 hours.

Preheat oven to 425 degrees F. Place meat in a roasting pan. Pour excess glaze into a small bowl and save for basting. Roast the pork 30 minutes undisturbed. Reduce oven temperature to 325 degrees F and continue roasting 1-1/4 hours, basting often with glaze. When an instant-read thermometer registers 145 degrees F, remove meat to a platter and allow to rest 10 to 15 minutes.

Place refrigerated glaze and cherry mixture in a small saucepan; warm over low temperature. Carve meat and serve with spoonfuls of warm Ancho-Cherry Glaze.

Note: Pork loin is generally considered the best cut for oven roasting. For more flavorful and moist meat, leave the bone in. Ask butcher to cut through the chine, or bottom, bone to make carving easier. Pork tenderloins, which are lower in fat than almost any other cut of meat, can also be used. Grilling or broiling a 1-1/4-pound tenderloin to an internal temperature of 145-degrees F takes about 10 to 15 minutes. (Tenderloins tend to be dry, so take care not to overcook.)

Herb and Scallion Polenta Spoonbread

This crunchy, crusted light spoonbread is infused with the bright, fresh flavors of herbs and scallions. Serve topped with "The City Different" Ratatouille (see p. 85) for a delicious light supper or lunch entrée.

Yield: 6 servings

1 tablespoon butter
1/2 cup sliced scallions (white bulbs and some green tops)
2 tablespoons minced fresh sage
1 tablespoon minced fresh parsley
1 teaspoon minced fresh thyme
Nonstick cooking spray
1 cup coarse ground yellow or white polenta
2 cups water
1 cup buttermilk
1 teaspoon salt
1/2 teaspoon white pepper
2 tablespoons butter, melted and cooled
3 egg yolks, beaten
2 teaspoons baking powder
3 egg whites
1/4 teaspoon cream of tartar

Preheat oven to 400 degrees F. Heat butter in a small frying pan over medium heat and sauté scallions until just starting to brown. Remove from heat and add sage, parsley and thyme. Spray a 10-inch cast-iron skillet with cooking spray and place in oven.

In a large saucepan, stir together polenta, water, buttermilk, salt and pepper. Bring to a boil, reduce heat to low, and cook slowly for 5 minutes, stirring constantly. Remove from heat and cool 10 minutes, stirring occasionally. Mix in scallions and herbs.

Whisk melted butter and egg yolks together, then stir in 1/2 cup polenta mixture. Using a heavy wooden spoon, combine egg mixture and baking powder with remaining polenta, stirring well. Beat egg whites and cream of tartar until stiff peaks form. Fold egg whites into polenta mixture. Remove heated skillet from oven and pour batter into skillet. Reduce temperature to 375 degrees F and return skillet to oven. Bake 35 minutes, or until top is golden brown. Serve immediately.

Variation: Add 1/2 cup roasted, peeled and chopped green chiles and 1 cup grated cheddar cheese to final mixture.

Sauté of Baby Summer Vegetables

Make this mélange of colorful vegetables at the height of summer when baby vegetables are at their best. If baby vegetables are unavailable, shred larger vegetables, and julienne the green beans.

Yield: 6 servings

2-1/2 tablespoons clarified butter or olive oil
9 thin baby carrots
2 shallots, minced
6 baby zucchini, quartered lengthwise
6 baby yellow crookneck squash, quartered lengthwise
1/2 pound very thin green beans
1 heaping tablespoon chopped fresh herbs (choose 3: marjoram, lemon thyme, savory, oregano, or opal basil)
Juice of 1/2 lemon
Salt and freshly ground pepper to taste

Clean and trim all vegetables. In a large skillet, heat butter or oil over medium-high heat. Add carrots and sauté 3 minutes. Add shallots and sauté 2 minutes. Add zucchini, squash and green beans; reduce heat to medium and cook 5 minutes, or until vegetables are crisp-tender. Stir in herbs and season with lemon juice, salt and pepper.

Variation: Highlight Santa Fe flavors by adding 2 teaspoons chile caribe (see p. 18) to salt and pepper.

Apple Tart in Phyllo Crust with Warm Cajeta Sauce

Apple pie is a favorite dessert whose popularity never wanes. This version is irresistible with its light flaky crust, flavorful apples, and rich caramel cajeta embellishment.

Yield: 6 to 8 servings

Crust:
6 tablespoons clarified butter, melted
8 sheets phyllo dough, thawed

Brush a 10-inch round springform pan lightly with butter. Lay 2 sheets of phyllo dough on a work surface to form a cross. With a pastry brush, lightly butter remaining sheets of phyllo as they are used; repeat layering procedure by arranging sheets at angles to form a circle. Using a foil-covered sheet of thin cardboard, gently lift phyllo into prepared pan and place on a baking sheet. Press phyllo into pan with fingertips and roll overhanging edges under loosely. Brush edge with remaining butter.

Filling:
4 baking apples, peeled, cored and sliced
1/8-inch thick
1 tablespoon lemon juice
6 tablespoons plus 1 tablespoon sugar
2 teaspoons ground canela
(or 1 teaspoon cinnamon)

1/4 teaspoon grated nutmeg
1/4 cup apple jelly, warmed slightly
1/4 cup chopped toasted almonds

Preheat oven to 350 degrees F. Place apples in a bowl and sprinkle with lemon juice, 6 tablespoons of sugar, canela and nutmeg. Toss gently until apples are coated. Spread apple jelly evenly on bottom of phyllo shell. Arrange apple slices over jelly in a decorative pattern. Sprinkle with almonds and remaining sugar. Bake 40 minutes, or until phyllo is golden and filling is bubbly. Remove from oven and increase oven temperature to 450 degrees F.

Topping:
1/2 cup vanilla yogurt
1 egg, beaten

Stir yogurt and egg together in a small bowl. Pour yogurt mixture over apples and return tart to oven. Bake 15 minutes, or until topping begins to brown. If the edges of the phyllo are getting too dark, cover them with foil. Cool at least 30 minutes before serving with Warm Cajeta Sauce.

Cajeta Sauce:
2 cups goat's milk
2 cups cow's milk
1 cup plus 2 tablespoons sugar
1 tablespoon corn syrup
1/4 teaspoon baking soda
1 teaspoon corn starch

Place milks, sugar, and corn syrup in a large heavy pan and bring to a simmer. Dissolve baking soda and corn starch in 2 tablespoons water and stir into milk mixture. (It will froth up but will stop when stirred.) Cook over medium-low heat 50 to 55 minutes, stirring occasionally, or until thickened and caramel-colored. Serve warm.

Note: For a truly delicious and indulgent dessert, serve Cajeta Sauce over cinnamon ice cream and apple tart. It is also good served with a fresh mango tart, bread pudding and baked apples. When refrigerated, rewarm in a double boiler until softened.

A Stargazers' Cookout

The altitude in Santa Fe ensures clear and bright conditions that are perfect for stargazers. The following menu will surely complement any astronomical experience with a galaxy of tastes and textures.

Seasonal Mixed Greens with Balsamic Dressing

Crisp pungent greens with a simple dressing are favored by many as the ideal salad to accompany a rich entrée. To give a less costly balsamic vinegar a flavor boost, add a teaspoon of brown sugar to a newly opened bottle and shake to mix.

Yield: 6 servings

Mixed Greens:
1 small bunch watercress
1 small head curly frisée
1 small head romaine lettuce (inner leaves only)
1/2 cup fresh basil leaves
1/4 cup fresh flat-leaf parsley leaves

Clean greens and tear into bite-sized pieces. Place greens and herbs in a large salad bowl. Pour enough Balsamic Dressing over salad to moisten; toss well.

Balsamic Dressing:
3 tablespoons red wine vinegar
3 tablespoons balsamic vinegar
2/3 cup extra virgin olive oil
1 teaspoon dark brown sugar
2 cloves garlic, finely chopped and sautéed in
　　1 teaspoon vegetable oil until translucent
Salt and pepper to taste

In a small saucepan, heat vinegars and olive oil; cook over moderate heat 2 minutes. Add brown sugar and simmer for 1 minute. Remove from heat and cool to room temperature. Add garlic and season with salt and pepper. At serving time, place in a small jar and shake well to blend.

Chile-Barbecued Salmon with Jalapeño, Herb and Orange Relish

This unbelievably flavorful salmon is equally appropriate for a backyard barbecue or a sophisticated dinner. The clean sharp flavors of the relish are perfect with the richly flavored salmon.

Yield: 6 servings

Chile Barbecue Sauce:
1 cup ketchup
1 cup honey
1/2 cup orange juice
1/4 cup whole-grain mustard
3 tablespoons ancho chile powder
2 tablespoons vinegar
2 teaspoons hot pepper sauce (or to taste)

2 teaspoons minced garlic
2 teaspoons olive oil
1 teaspoon Worcestershire sauce
1 teaspoon soy sauce
1 teaspoon toasted and ground cumin
1 teaspoon ground canela
    (or 1/2 teaspoon cinnamon)

Combine sauce ingredients in a small heavy saucepan and heat to a simmer. Cook 2 minutes, stirring occasionally. Chill in refrigerator before using.

Salmon:
6 (6-ounce) salmon fillets
Salt and pepper

Preheat a gas or charcoal grill to medium high. Season salmon with salt and pepper; brush both sides generously with sauce. Grill on a well-oiled rack 3 minutes on each side, brushing frequently with sauce, until salmon is done to your taste. Serve each fillet with a sprinkle of Jalapeño, Herb and Orange Relish.

Jalapeño, Herb and Orange Relish:
3 tablespoons chopped fresh Italian parsley
1 tablespoon chopped fresh cilantro
2 tablespoons grated orange peel
2 jalapeños, stemmed, seeded and chopped
1 teaspoon rice vinegar

Mix all ingredients together in a small bowl. Taste and adjust seasonings as necessary.

Oven-Roasted Corn
with Chipotle Aioli
and Tomato-Basil Butter

Fresh corn is one of the greatest pleasures of summer. This easy process of oven roasting produces crunchy sweet corn. Serve corn on a platter with bowls of spreads and dips.

Yield: 6 servings

6 or more ears of corn, husks and silks removed

Preheat oven to 450 degrees F. Place corn directly on oven rack and cook until tender. Roasting time will depend upon size of ears of corn, usually about 12 to 15 minutes. Cut ears of corn into thirds and serve with small bowls of

Chipotle Aioli and Tomato-Basil Butter or Dry Chile Dunk and Seasoned Citrus Salt (see p. 42).

Chipotle Aioli:
1/4 cup chipotles en adobo with sauce (see p. 18)
3 egg yolks
2 teaspoons Dijon mustard
1/2 teaspoon coarse salt
2 cloves garlic, minced
1 tablespoon cider vinegar
1 teaspoon lemon juice
1/2 cup olive oil

In a food processor, combine first 7 ingredients and pulse to combine. With motor running, add olive oil in a slow steady stream until mixture is thickened. Taste for seasonings.

Tomato-Basil Butter:
1 stick cold butter or margarine, cut into chunks
1/4 cup drained, chopped sun-dried tomatoes
    packed in oil
1 tablespoon coarsely chopped fresh basil leaves
Salt and pepper to taste

Pulse in a food processor just until blended.

Rosy Wine and Raspberry-Poached Peaches

Use unblemished yellow peaches at their peak of ripeness for this delicious light summer dessert. The rosy-hued peaches and raspberries need no further embellishment.

Yield: 6 servings
2 (10-ounce) packages unsweetened frozen
    raspberries, drained
1 tablespoon lemon juice
1 cup sugar
1 bottle red wine, such as Zinfandel or Pinot Noir
12 small whole peaches, peeled, cut in half
    and pitted
1 pint fresh raspberries

In a food processor or blender, combine raspberries and lemon juice; process until puréed. Strain through a fine mesh sieve and discard seeds. Place purée in a large non-reactive saucepan and add sugar and wine. Bring to a boil and add peaches. Reduce heat to low and poach peaches 2 minutes.

Using a slotted spoon, transfer peaches to a bowl. Bring poaching liquid to a boil; cook until liquid is reduced to about 1-1/2 cups. Cool slightly, then pour over peaches. Cover and refrigerate until cold, at least 2 hours. Turn peaches occasionally as they are chilling. Serve in clear glass bowls topped with fresh raspberries.

A Constellation of Chocolate-Dipped Fruits

To conclude a memorable evening under the stars, why not serve your guests one last little sweet to enjoy with their final cups of coffee? These chocolates will brighten the evening and make a marvelous lasting impression.

Yield: 24 to 36 pieces, depending on size of fruits used
6 ounces high-quality semisweet chocolate
1 tablespoon unsalted butter
1/2 teaspoon ground canela
    (or 1/4 teaspoon ground cinnamon)
Assorted fruits (pineapple chunks, dried apricots,
    orange segments with membranes removed,
    2-inch-long slices of fresh coconut, strawberries
    with stems attached, washed and dried)
Wooden skewers

Combine chocolate, butter, and canela in a double boiler over moderate heat. Melt chocolate, stirring frequently, until smooth.* Remove from heat. (Chocolate can be melted in a microwave oven on low power, stirring every 15 seconds until melted.)

Cover a large baking sheet with waxed paper. Working quickly, hold the strawberries by their stems or hulls and dip each one into chocolate mixture, covering about 2/3 of the berry. Place coated berries on waxed paper to cool and harden. Repeat with other fruits, impaling them on the ends of skewers to dip into chocolate. Store dipped fruits in a cool place for up to 8 hours. (They may be stored overnight in the refrigerator, layered between waxed paper in a tightly sealed container.)

*Do not let any drops of water get into the melted chocolate or it will be gritty. Dry fresh fruits completely before dipping in chocolate.

CHEF'S CORNER: *To finish ripening stone fruits such as peaches, apricots, and plums, place them in a loosely closed paper bag overnight.*

¡Fiesta!

A Fiesta Brunch Buffet

Stacked Tortilla and Chorizo Omelets with Roasted

Tomato-Chile Sauce • Potato and Cheese Enchiladas with

Green Chile Sauce • Black Beans with Three-Herb Topping • Grilled and

Chilled Cactus Salad • Apple Capirotada

A Historical Parade Party

Crisp Chicken Flautas and Baby Spinach-Radicchio-Pear

Salad with Spicy Balsamic Vinaigrette • Fiesta Carne Adovada

Burritos • Drunken Beans • Natillas Nuevas with

Coffee Custard Sauce

A "Zozobra Burns" Buffet

Diced Vegetable Salad Boats with Santa Fe Vinaigrette • Grilled

Adobo Pork Chops • Mixed Vegetable Grill • Fresh

Lime Ice Cream • Biscochitos

Fiesta! The word alone conjures a sense of excitement, good times, and great food!

Historically, Fiestas de Santa Fe was the most exhilarating week of the year in sleepy remote Santa Fe. Preparation for the parades and events started months in advance—fiesta dresses were sewn by local dressmakers who pulled their bolts of colorful fabric down from the storage areas next to the vigas, floats were built and decorated, events organized. Yet Fiestas de Santa Fe is more than a holiday. It is a celebration of faith and family and Hispanic culture.

The week-long whirl of parades, parties and events commemorates the return of the Spanish to the city in 1692 under the leadership of Don Diego de Vargas. Twelve years before, the Pueblo Indians had evicted the Spanish from New Mexico in a battle called the Pueblo Revolt.

Festivities start with a colorful ritual, the burning of Zozobra, a three-story-tall mechanized puppet that represents Old Man Gloom. Thousands gather in and around Fort Marcy Park—on rooftops, balconies, even in trees—to get a good vantage point for this event, which takes place at dusk. Families arrive well in advance, bringing a picnic spread to better enjoy the festivities. Bands entertain the crowds as the excitement builds; costumed dancers bound about the stage with torches, stirring up the audience before lighting the huge puppet. Zozobra sways back and forth, flailing his arms and groaning as onlookers chant, "Burn him! Burn him!" Finally, to much applause, Zozobra is burned and gloom is considered dispelled for the coming year.

Desfiles de los Niños, or Children's Pet Parade, is the first official parade of the week. There, children dressed up in costumes of all kinds march down city thoroughfares with their pets, which are elaborately attired as well. Poodles dyed pink for the occasion and sporting berets walk alongside bulldogs in boas and mutts bedecked with sparkling fairy wings. Cats in hot pants pad along next to their two-legged, four-legged and feathered friends on the parade route.

The Historical/Hysterical Parade is another event not to be missed. Elaborately costumed Spanish conquistadors lead the parade on horseback. Don Diego de Vargas and his queen, replete in silk and velvet garments trimmed with lace and gold, cruise by on a spectacular float with their many attendants. Other historical figures march behind, as do a number of local high school marching bands, local business groups, clubs, and other performers.

Closing ceremonies commence with an evening mass at the historic St. Francis Cathedral. After mass, the faithful carry lighted candles and form a procession to the Cross of the Martyrs. It is a beautiful sight—participants create waves of light in the darkness as they wind their way slowly through town.

Add to the mix a Grand Ball, some excellent mariachi concerts, arts and crafts markets, entertainment on the Plaza, and you'll get an idea of Fiesta, the event that marks the unofficial end of summer in Santa Fe.

A Fiesta Brunch Buffet

Think mariachi bands in sombreros and studded pants, strumming their melodious guitars; flamenco dancers in colorful costumes, swirling and stamping their feet to an infectious Latin rhythm; parades, parties, feasts and fun—the whirl that is Fiesta! The week is one long tribute to the highlights of Hispanic culture, with celebratory brunches and buffets aplenty.

Stacked Tortilla and Chorizo Omelets with Roasted Tomato-Chile Sauce

Chorizo is a spiced Mexican pork sausage that adds zing to this dish. The Santa Fe Farmers' Market features many vendors who sell farm-fresh eggs. Try to find locally fresh eggs, as they make a world of difference to the taste of omelets. The Roasted Tomato-Chile Sauce lends a fresh piquancy to the dish.

Yield: 6 to 8 servings

Stacked Tortilla and Chorizo Omelets:
9 extra large eggs
3 tablespoons water
3 serrano or jalapeño chiles, stemmed, seeded and finely diced
1/2 cup sliced scallions, green tops included
1 cup pork or beef chorizo (or other bulk sausage), cooked and well drained
Salt and freshly ground pepper
Butter
4 (8- to 10-inch) flour tortillas
2-1/2 cups warm Roasted Tomato-Chile Sauce
3/4 cup grated Monterey Jack or queso fresco

CHEF'S CORNER: *Cold eggs produce tough omelets and scrambled eggs. Use eggs at room temperature, or place cold eggs in a bowl of hot tap water for five minutes.*

Beat eggs with water and stir in chiles, scallions, chorizo, salt and pepper. Melt butter in an 8- to 10-inch nonstick frying pan over medium-low heat; cook omelets in 4 batches to make 4 flat omelets.

Preheat oven to 350 degrees F. Generously butter an oven-proof serving dish. Place an omelet on the dish, cover with a tortilla, spoon on about 1/4 cup of Roasted Tomato-Chile Sauce, and sprinkle with cheese. Repeat layering, ending with cheese. Bake for 10 minutes, or until cheese is melted and omelets are well heated. Allow to set 5 minutes; cut into wedges and serve with remaining sauce.

Roasted Tomato-Chile Sauce (2 cups):

10 Roma tomatoes, roasted and peeled (see p. 26), or 1 (28-ounce) can of quality-canned tomatoes, drained

3 jalapeños, stemmed and roughly chopped
1/2 cup chopped white onion
1 large clove garlic, roughly chopped
1/2 teaspoon toasted and ground cumin
1/2 teaspoon dried Mexican oregano
1 tablespoon vegetable oil
Salt to taste

Roughly chop tomatoes and place in a blender or food processor. Add remaining ingredients except oil and salt. Process mixture until smooth.

Heat oil in a heavy saucepot over medium-high heat until almost smoking. Add sauce all at once and continue cooking 5 minutes, stirring constantly. Lower heat and simmer until sauce has thickened. Season with salt.

Potato and Cheese Enchiladas with Green Chile Sauce

These enchiladas, stuffed with potatoes and a variety of cheeses, are a tasty contemporary version of traditional enchiladas. New Mexico green chiles can be very hot, so use Anaheims or a mixture of the two if a milder green chile sauce is desired.

Yield: 8 servings

Potato and Cheese Enchiladas:
8 medium red potatoes, unpeeled
2 tablespoons canola oil
**1 large white onion, cut in half and
    very thinly sliced**
3 jalapeño chiles, minced
1/4 cup chopped fresh cilantro
4 ounces Monterey Jack or Muenster cheese, grated
4 ounces mild goat cheese, cut into small cubes
2 teaspoons salt
Vegetable oil
8 (8-inch) blue or yellow corn tortillas

Boil potatoes in water until cooked but still firm; drain. While still warm, peel and cut potatoes into 1/2-inch dice. Heat oil in a large heavy skillet and fry potatoes until lightly browned. Add onion and sauté until softened. Stir in chiles and cilantro.

Preheat oven to 350 degrees F and lightly oil a 9 x 12-inch baking dish. Add oil to a medium frying pan and heat until almost smoking. Quickly fry tortillas in hot oil for a few seconds on each side, or until pliable. Drain and blot on paper towels.

Green Chile Sauce (about 4 cups):
**3 cups roasted, peeled, and diced New Mexico
    green chiles**
1 cup diced onion
2 cloves garlic, finely chopped
3 tablespoons corn oil
2 tablespoons flour
**2 teaspoons chopped fresh oregano leaves
    (or 1 teaspoon dried Mexican oregano)**
1 teaspoon toasted and ground coriander seed
1-1/2 cups chicken broth
Salt to taste
1 tablespoon chopped fresh cilantro leaves (optional)

Sauté onion and garlic in oil over medium heat until softened. Stir in flour; continue cooking and stirring 1 minute. Whisk in broth and add remaining ingredients except cilantro. Simmer sauce 15 minutes, covered, stirring occasionally. Add cilantro and taste to adjust seasoning.

Note: This recipe will make more sauce than is needed for the enchiladas. It freezes well and has many uses—on burritos, eggs, tostadas, potatoes and as a base for green chile stews and soups. Frozen green chiles can be used, but the flavor (and the aroma in your kitchen!) is better with freshly roasted green chiles.

To assemble: Pour 1 cup Green Chile Sauce in a baking dish and distribute evenly on the bottom. Pour remaining sauce in a shallow bowl. Pass each tortilla through sauce to coat lightly; place on a baking sheet. Spoon potato filling on tortillas and sprinkle cheeses on top, reserving 3 tablespoons of Monterey Jack cheese. Roll tortillas into cylinders and place seam side down in baking dish. Spoon reserved sauce liberally over enchiladas and sprinkle with reserved cheese. Bake 15 minutes, or until enchiladas are hot and cheeses are melted.

Black Beans
with Three-Herb Topping

These well-seasoned beans with vegetables are fragrant with fresh herbs. Anise seeds lend a subtle hint of licorice.

Yield: 8 servings

Black Beans:
1/2 pound dried black beans, cleaned and
    soaked overnight in water
Vegetable oil
1 medium white onion, chopped
2 medium carrots, chopped
2 celery stalks, chopped
4 large cloves garlic, minced
2 bay leaves
1 tablespoon chopped fresh thyme
2 teaspoons anise seed
2 tablespoons chopped fresh rosemary
8 cups water
Salt
Juice of 1 lime

Heat oil in a large heavy pot; cook vegetables, herbs and spices over low heat until tender, about 15 minutes. Add beans to the pot along with enough water to cover. Bring to a boil, reduce heat, cover and simmer until beans are soft, stirring and adding water occasionally. Add salt and lime juice to taste. Serve in small cups topped with Three-Herb Topping.

Three-Herb Topping (1 cup):
1/2 cup packed fresh cilantro leaves, finely chopped
1/4 cup packed fresh mint leaves, finely chopped
1/4 cup packed fresh Italian parsley leaves,
    finely chopped
1-1/2 teaspoons garlic, minced
1/2 teaspoon salt
3 serrano chiles or jalapeños, stemmed, seeded
    and minced
1 tablespoon extra virgin olive oil
1 tablespoon fresh lime juice

Place all ingredients in a small bowl; stir to combine.

Grilled and Chilled Cactus Salad

Nopales, the tender pads of the prickly pear cactus, are harvested in southern New Mexico in early summer. Their flavor is reminiscent of a tart green bell pepper crossed with a green bean. Grilling fresh nopales greatly enhances their tangy vegetable flavor without softening the texture. Wrapped in a tortilla or lettuce leaf, this salad also makes a tasty vegetarian taco or burrito.

Yield: 6 to 8 servings

1-1/2 pounds cleaned nopales (see p. 25)
Vegetable oil
Salt
Juice from 1 small fresh lime
12 cherry tomatoes, halved if large
1 cup dry-roasted corn (see p. 25)
2 jalapeños, stemmed, seeded and finely diced
4 tablespoons chopped scallions
1 tablespoon chopped cilantro
1/4 cup white wine vinegar
1 teaspoon salt
1/2 teaspoon freshly ground black pepper
1/2 teaspoon dried sage leaves, crumbled
1/2 cup olive oil
Red lettuce leaves

Score each side of nopales 3 or 4 times with a knife. Brush with vegetable oil and sprinkle with salt and lime juice. Grill over medium-low charcoal fire 15 to 20 minutes, turning occasionally (or roast 20 minutes on a griddle heated to medium-low, turning occasionally). Cool and cut into 1/4-inch strips; chill 2 hours or overnight.

In a large bowl, combine nopales, tomatoes, corn, jalapeños, scallions and cilantro. Shake vinegar, salt, pepper, sage and oil in a small jar until mixed. Pour over nopales and toss well. Serve on a platter lined with lettuce leaves.

CHEF'S CORNER: *In a hurry? Too busy to spend extra time in the kitchen? Substitute canned nopales for fresh ones in any recipe; they only require rinsing before using.*

Apple Capirotada

This candy-rich pudding was originally served in northern New Mexico for special holidays. Eggs were eliminated from the traditional bread pudding recipes used in other areas, and cheese was added. In this contemporary version, cream cheese is used instead of the usual Cheddar or Monterey Jack cheese.

Yield: 10 to 12 servings

12 ounces French bread, cut into small cubes
6 tablespoons unsalted butter, melted
1-1/2 cups brown sugar
3-1/4 cups water
2 cloves
1 stick canela or cinnamon
2 cups peeled and chopped baking apples
1/4 cup raisins
1/2 cup chopped pecans, walnuts or piñon nuts
8 ounces cream cheese, cut into small cubes
Heavy cream

Preheat oven to 350 degrees F. Butter a 9 x 13-inch baking pan and set aside. Place bread in a large bowl, drizzle with butter, and toss until well coated. Toast bread on a baking sheet for 15 minutes, turning occasionally, or until crisp and lightly browned.

Combine brown sugar, water, cloves and canela in a saucepan; bring to a boil. Lower heat and simmer about 15 minutes, or until mixture is slightly thickened and reduced by one-fourth. Remove cloves and canela after syrup has cooled slightly. Layer half the bread cubes in the prepared baking pan, top with half the apples, raisins, nuts and cream cheese. Drizzle with half the syrup; repeat layering with remaining ingredients. Using a wide spatula, gently press bread mixture into syrup, making sure it is well soaked. Bake 25 minutes, or until top is golden brown and syrup is absorbed. Serve warm with heavy cream.

Variation: Experiment by using 1 cup of any dried fruit in place of fresh apples; use mild Cheddar or Monterey Jack cheese for cream cheese.

A Historical Parade Party

One of the highlights of Fiestas de Santa Fe is the Historical/Hysterical Parade, an event that celebrates the re-conquest of Santa Fe by Don Diego de Vargas in 1692. Elaborately dressed, de Vargas and his queen, La Reina, lead the parade with a number of costumed conquistadors in attendance. Singers, dancers, and school bands also follow the route, making for a fun and festive day.

Crisp Chicken Flautas and Baby Spinach-Radicchio-Pear Salad with Spicy Balsamic Vinaigrette

Flautas, or "flutes," are corn tortillas that have been rolled around a filling into a cigar-like form and fried. Also known as taquitos, these crisp treats originated in Mexico and are made with a variety of fillings. A contrast of textures and flavors—sweet, tart, spicy, crisp and soft—are presented in this visually appealing starter. Substitute refried beans for chicken to make flavorful vegetarian flautas.

Yield: 12 flautas

Filling:
1 pound cooked boneless, skinless
    chicken breasts, shredded
1 tablespoon vegetable oil
2 cloves garlic, minced
2 teaspoons dried Mexican oregano
1 teaspoon toasted and ground coriander seeds
1 teaspoon salt
2 pickled jalapeño chiles, chopped

Heat oil over medium heat in a large skillet and sauté garlic, stirring, until softened. Add chicken and remaining ingredients. Stir-fry until chicken is lightly browned. Set aside.

Note: Cut this recipe in half if you prefer to serve only one flauta on each salad plate.

Tortillas:
12 (8-inch) yellow or blue corn tortillas
Vegetable oil

Preheat oven to 325 degrees F. Wrap tortillas, 6 to a stack, in aluminum foil and heat in oven 5 minutes. Working with 1 tortilla at a time (keep others wrapped to stay warm), spoon 3 tablespoons of filling down the center of each tortilla, roll into a tight cylinder, and close seam with a toothpick. Repeat rolling and sealing with remaining tortillas and filling.

Line a rack with paper towels. Heat 4 inches of oil in a heavy skillet until sizzling but not smoking. Using tongs, fry flautas in batches 3 to 5 minutes, until golden and crisp. Transfer to rack to drain. Remove toothpicks and cut flautas in half on the diagonal with a serrated knife.

Baby Spinach-Radicchio-Pear Salad:
6 cups packed baby spinach leaves
1/2 cup radicchio leaves, torn into bite-sized pieces
2 pears, peeled and cubed
1 small red onion, sliced paper-thin, rinsed and dried

Toss spinach, radicchio and pears in a large bowl with enough Spicy Balsamic Vinaigrette to coat.

Spicy Balsamic Vinaigrette:
6 tablespoons olive oil
2 tablespoons balsamic vinegar
1 teaspoon toasted and lightly crushed
coriander seeds
1 teaspoon sugar (less if vinegar is sweet)
1/2 teaspoon cayenne pepper

Combine all ingredients in a small bowl and whisk together until well combined.

To serve: Stand flautas in middle of serving plate, circle with salad, and garnish with red onion slices.

Note: Flautas can be prepared 24 hours ahead, wrapped air-tight in plastic wrap and refrigerated. Bring to room temperature before frying. They are also good served with Crunchy Garden Vegetable Salsa or Tomatillo Guacamole (see p. 31) on beds of shredded lettuce or cabbage. For a reduced-fat version, bake flautas on a large baking sheet for 6 minutes at 400 degrees F, until lightly browned and crisp. Flautas are often eaten as finger foods.

Fiesta Carne Adovada Burritos

This New Mexico "soul food," considered a mainstay of Santa Fe cuisine, is frequently served in homes, restaurants and on feast days. Adovada features meat, typically pork, in a thick red-chile-based sauce that is generally quite spicy. Marinating the meat overnight and simmering it slowly in the oven ensures that it will be tender and rich in flavor.

Yield: 8 burritos

Filling:
2-1/2 pounds pork loin or Boston butt,
    trimmed and cut into bite-sized pieces
1 tablespoon vegetable oil

Heat oil in a large heavy skillet over medium-high heat; brown meat in several batches. Set aside.

Adovada Sauce:
1/2 pound (about 20 to 25) whole dried
    New Mexico red chiles (preferably Chimayo
    chiles),* stemmed, seeded and rinsed
2 dried ancho chiles, stemmed, seeded and rinsed
    (see p. 15)
2 tablespoons vegetable oil
1 medium white onion, chopped
4 cloves garlic, chopped
2-1/2 cups beef or chicken stock or water
1 tablespoon cider vinegar

1/2 cup freshly squeezed orange juice
1 tablespoon brown sugar
2 teaspoons dried Mexican oregano
1 teaspoon toasted and freshly ground coriander
1 teaspoon toasted and freshly ground cumin
1 teaspoon ground canela
Salt to taste

8 flour tortillas, warm

Preheat oven to 300 degrees F. Oil a large oven-proof baking dish. Toast chiles in a dry cast-iron skillet about 2 minutes, or until they have darkened slightly. (They burn very easily, so watch carefully and turn frequently.) Place toasted chiles in a large bowl and cover with hot water. Place a plate on top of chiles to keep them submerged; allow to sit for 30 minutes.

Transfer chiles and some soaking liquid to a blender. Purée until very smooth, adding enough liquid to produce a smooth, sauce-like mixture. Reserve any remaining liquid. (It is easiest to purée chiles in several batches.)

Heat oil in a large saucepan over medium-high heat. Sauté onions until golden brown; stir in garlic and sauté briefly. Add browned meat, chile purée, stock, vinegar, orange juice, brown sugar, oregano, coriander, cumin and canela; stir well to combine. (At this point, you can refrigerate the Carne Adovada overnight or proceed with cooking.)

Place meat mixture in prepared baking dish, cover and bake until meat is tender and sauce has been reduced, about 1-1/2 hours. Stir occasionally, adding some reserved soaking liquid if sauce seems too dry. Add salt the last 15 minutes of cooking; if sauce is too thin, uncover baking dish to finish cooking. Serve meat wrapped in warm flour tortillas.

*Any dried red chiles will work in this recipe, but for the best balance of sweet and heat, dried Chimayo red chiles are the choice. (For ordering information, see Local Sources on page 144.)

Drunken Beans

Pinto beans are one of the cornerstones of New Mexico cuisine. They are in season from May through November, making them one of the highest-yielding crops in the area. They are also an excellent source of protein and have historically been served here in place of meat. These beans, simmered in Mexican beer, have a unique and hearty flavor.

Yield: 6 to 8 servings

2 tablespoons peanut or vegetable oil

1 large white onion, chopped

3 cloves garlic, minced

2 cups pinto beans, cleaned, rinsed, soaked 4 hours or overnight, and drained

1 smoked pork shank (optional)

2 dried chipotle chiles

2 teaspoons dried Mexican oregano

1 teaspoon dried thyme

1 teaspoon toasted and ground cumin seeds

1 bay leaf

6 cups of water, plus additional as necessary

1 (12-ounce) bottle dark Mexican beer, water, or beef stock

2 teaspoons salt (or to taste)

In a large heavy pot, sauté onion in oil until lightly browned. Add garlic and sauté briefly. Add remaining ingredients except salt and bring to a boil. Reduce heat to low and cook until beans are soft, about 2 hours; if beans begin to dry out, add water during cooking. Add salt the last 10 minutes of cooking. Remove pork shank, shred and mix with beans, or save for another use.

Natillas Nuevas
with Coffee Custard Sauce

*Traditionally **natillas**, or custards, were thickened with a little cornstarch or flour to save on eggs. Natillas Nuevas, a contemporary version of a floating island dessert, is beautifully light and delicious. Make the coffee-flavored sauce ahead so that it can be served ice cold.*

Yield: 6 servings

Caramel:
1-1/4 cups sugar

Heat a large, heavy dry skillet over moderate heat; add sugar and swirl in skillet over heat until melted. Continue cooking, using a wooden spatula to press any unmelted sugar to center of pan until a dark golden caramel forms. Carefully pour into a 9-1/2-inch ring mold, rotating it quickly to coat sides before caramel sets. Cool.

Meringue:
6 large egg whites, room temperature
1/4 teaspoon cream of tartar
1/2 cup sugar
1 teaspoon pure vanilla extract

Preheat oven to 275 degrees F. With an electric mixer, beat egg whites until soft peaks are formed. Gradually add cream of tartar, sugar and vanilla; continue beating until whites are very stiff and glossy.

Spoon mixture into mold, removing any air pockets by rapping mold sharply on a hard surface. Place uncovered mold in a larger pan containing hot water that comes halfway up the sides of the mold. Bake 1 hour, or until meringue is firm and pale brown on top.

Remove from oven and quickly run a wet knife around the edge of the mold. Holding a serving plate over the mold, immediately invert. Dribble any remaining caramel over the meringue. The meringue can be made up to 8 hours ahead and kept cool at room temperature.

Coffee Custard Sauce:
2 cups half-and-half, divided
6 large egg yolks
1/2 cup sugar
1 teaspoon pure vanilla extract
3 tablespoons coffee liqueur

Warm 1 cup of half-and-half in a small heavy saucepan over low heat. Beat remaining cup of half-and-half with egg yolks and sugar in a small bowl until well combined. Add warmed cream in a thin stream to egg mixture, whisking constantly. Return mixture to saucepan and cook over low-medium heat, stirring constantly with a wooden spoon until sauce resembles heavy cream (175 degrees F on a candy thermometer). Do not allow to boil or it will curdle. Immediately remove from heat and stir in vanilla and liqueur. Transfer to a bowl and refrigerate until serving time.

To serve: Pour Coffee Custard Sauce into small individual serving bowls and top with large spoonfuls of meringue.

A "Zozobra Burns" Buffet

Zozobra, or Old Man Gloom, has been burned for decades here as an opener for fiesta festivities. It is as big a night for entertaining in Santa Fe as is New Year's Eve and there are parties all over town. Those people with homes overlooking Fort Marcy Park that have the best views of Zozobra are usually the willing hosts of a festive dinner served after Old Man Gloom has perished.

Diced Vegetable Salad Boats with Santa Fe Vinaigrette

This salad can also be served as an appetizer by standing the lettuce leaves, stem ends down, in a bowl half-filled with ice cubes. Toss the diced vegetables with the dressing just before serving and place in a bowl nearby so they can be scooped up with the crisp lettuce leaves.

Yield: 6 servings

Diced Vegetable Salad Boats:
1 large head romaine lettuce, inner leaves only, cleaned and trimmed
3 cups assorted diced vegetables (avocados, red and yellow tomatoes, cucumbers, radishes, scallions, jalapeño chiles, and red, yellow and green bell peppers)

Arrange lettuce leaves on a large platter and place spoonfuls of diced vegetables on each leaf. Drizzle with Santa Fe Vinaigrette just before serving.

Santa Fe Vinaigrette:
2 Roma tomatoes, halved
2 jalapeño chiles, cut in half lengthwise, stemmed and seeded
2 cloves garlic, unpeeled
1/2 cup olive oil
1/4 cup red wine vinegar
2 tablespoons chopped fresh oregano
1 tablespoon chopped fresh cilantro or parsley
1/4 teaspoon freshly toasted and ground cumin
Salt and pepper to taste

Preheat oven to 450 degrees F. Place tomatoes, jalapeños and garlic, cut sides down, in a small foil-lined roasting pan. Brush lightly with a little oil. Roast until well browned, about 15 minutes. Remove from oven and cool.

Pull skins from tomatoes and garlic; place tomatoes, garlic and chiles in a blender or food processor. Add vinegar and any accumulated juices from roasting pan. Purée until smooth, then add remaining oil in a slow stream with the motor running. Add oregano, parsley and cumin; pulse to combine. Season with salt and pepper.

Grilled Adobo Pork Chops

Adobo is the Southwest's answer to barbecue sauce and can be used for lamb, chicken and brisket. The pork chops are glazed with a spicy crust on the outside and infused with complex rich flavors inside.

Yield: 6 servings

Marinade:
1/4 cup vegetable oil
1/4 cup chopped garlic
3 tablespoons ancho chile powder
3 tablespoons New Mexico chile powder
    (mild, medium, or hot)
1 tablespoon chipotle chile powder
1/2 teaspoon ground canela
    (or 1/4 teaspoon cinnamon)
2 cups drained canned tomatoes
2 tablespoons dark molasses
3 tablespoons red wine vinegar

Heat oil in a medium saucepan over moderate heat and sauté garlic until limp. Add chile powders and continue stirring 1 minute. Add remaining ingredients, stir, and simmer 10 minutes over very low heat. Cool to room temperature and purée in a food processor until smooth.

Grilled Pork Chops:
6 loin pork chops, 1-inch thick

Combine pork chops with marinade in a shallow glass pan; marinate 4 hours or overnight in the refrigerator.

Preheat grill or broiler to moderate heat. Remove meat from marinade, shaking off excess. Save remaining marinade for basting. Grill or broil chops 10 minutes, or to your preferred level of doneness, turning frequently and basting with marinade during last few minutes.

Mixed Vegetable Grill

Grilling vegetables produces an outstanding, slightly charred flavor. They look particularly attractive when piled high on one large serving platter.

Yield: 6 servings

Vinaigrette:
1/4 cup olive oil
3 tablespoons lemon juice
2 tablespoons balsamic vinegar
1 teaspoon Dijon mustard
1/2 teaspoon salt
1/2 teaspoon freshly ground black pepper

Shake all ingredients together in a small jar until well combined.

Vegetables:
3 medium russet potatoes, scrubbed and cut into
    1/2-inch-thick rounds
12 large scallions with green tops, trimmed
3 ears corn, husked, silks removed and cut into
    2-inch rounds
2 large poblano chiles
2 red bell peppers

Prepare a charcoal grill or preheat broiler for moderate heat. Brush potatoes, scallions and corn lightly on both sides with vinaigrette; place vegetables, chiles and peppers on grill rack. Turn frequently, brushing occasionally with vinaigrette. When chiles and peppers are charred all around, remove to a cutting board, cover and let cool.

Remove other vegetables to a serving platter as they are cooked. (They will each require different cooking times and must be watched carefully.) Peel and seed cooled peppers. Slice into 1/4-inch strips and transfer to serving platter. Pour any remaining vinaigrette over vegetables; serve at room temperature.

Note: Place chiles and peppers directly over the heat source so they can char quickly. Other vegetables should be cooked over indirect heat.

Fresh Lime Ice Cream

This refreshing ice cream, with its sweet and tangy flavor, is a perfect cool ending to a fiery Zozobra celebration.

Yield: 1-1/2 quarts
1 tablespoon grated lime peel, packed
1/2 cup plus 1 tablespoon fresh lime juice
2 cups superfine sugar
Pinch of salt
2 cups heavy cream
2 cups whole milk

In a large bowl, combine lime peel, juice, sugar and salt; mix well. Slowly pour in cream and then milk, stirring until sugar dissolves. Refrigerate for a minimum of 4 hours. (This ice cream is best when mixture is allowed to develop

its full flavor in the refrigerator overnight.) Stir mixture before pouring into ice-cream maker; freeze according to manufacturer's directions. Serve with biscochitos.

Biscochitos

Biscochitos have the honor of being the state cookie of New Mexico. Historically associated with Christmas, these tender anise-flavored cookies are now favorites in Santa Fe all year long. Vegetable shortening can be substituted for lard, but the flaky texture and flavor will be less luxurious.

Yield: 5 dozen 2-inch-diameter cookies
Topping:
1/4 cup sugar
1-1/2 teaspoons canela (or 1 teaspoon cinnamon)

Mix and set aside.

Cookies:
2 cups lard or vegetable shortening
1-1/2 cups sugar
2 eggs
1/4 cup sweet wine or brandy
1 tablespoon anise seeds, lightly crushed
6 cups flour
1 tablespoon baking powder
1 teaspoon salt

Preheat oven to 350 degrees F. Using an electric mixer, cream lard and sugar until light and fluffy. Add eggs, wine and anise seeds, beating until smooth. Sift flour, baking powder and salt together; stir into wet ingredients. Refrigerate dough for 15 minutes.

Divide dough in half. On a lightly floured pastry board, roll out dough 1/4 inch thick. Cut into decorative shapes with a cookie cutter. Place cookies on ungreased or parchment-covered baking sheets; sprinkle lightly with sugar topping. Bake about 10 minutes, or until lightly browned. Remove cookies to a rack lined with paper towels; sprinkle with remaining topping.

Local Sources for Southwestern Ingredients, Goods and Equipment

Coyote Café General Store

132 West Water Street
Santa Fe, NM 85501
(800) 866-4695 toll-free
www.coyote-café.com
— **A gourmet food store offering a variety of
regional cookbooks, salsas, hot sauces, food
items and Coyote Café logo clothing.**

Native Seeds/Search

526 North Fourth Avenue
Tucson, AZ 85705
(520) 327-9123 catalog or information
(520) 327-5821 fax or mail orders
— **Nonprofit organization that works to preserve
traditional crops and wild foodstuffs in the
Southwest and northern Mexico. Specializes
in seed, beans, grains, herbs and spices, and
educational materials on cooking, indigenous
agriculture and ethnobotany.**

Pueblo Harvest Foods

P.O. Box 1188
San Juan Pueblo, NM 87566
(888) 511-1120 toll-free
www.puebloharvest.com
— **Offers "Pueblo Harvest" line of Native American and gourmet foods as well as gift items that reflect the community's rich cultural traditions.**

Santa Fe School of Cooking and Market

116 West San Francisco Street
Santa Fe, NM 87501
(800) 982-4688 toll-free
(505) 983-4511
www.santafeschoolofcooking.com
— **Offers cooking classes and market items that include more than twenty varieties of dried chiles and powders, chipotle chiles in adobo, herbs, spices, posole, specialty cooking equipment and more.**

The Chile Shop

109 East Water Street
Santa Fe, NM 87501
(505) 983-6080
(505) 984-0737 fax
www.thechileshop.com
— **Offers a variety of chile powders, corn products, cookbooks, and household items, "everything needed for the flavor of the Southwest."**

Index